WHAT DO THEY SEEK?

Explorers, adventurers, scientists. Men and women who always broadened the horizons, for all humankind to share. Rolex was at their side when they reached the deepest point in the oceans, the highest summits of the Earth, the deepest jungles and both poles. But now that we know, more than ever, that our world has its limits, why do they continue to venture out there, again and again? Certainly not for kudos, accolades, or an ephemeral record. What they truly seek is to understand more intimately how complex and delicate our planet is, to document its change and how together, we can affect it for the better. So as long as they need it, we will be at their side. Because today, the real discovery is not so much about finding new lands. It's about looking with new eyes at the marvels of our planet, rekindling our sense of wonder, and acting to preserve our pale blue dot in the universe…
Doing our very best for a Perpetual Planet.

#Perpetual

OYSTER PERPETUAL
ROLEX DEEPSEA

ROLEX

Will the world always be this unpredictable?

Will my investments weather the storm?
How can I be sure?

 UBS

**For some of life's questions, you're not alone.
Together we can find an answer.**

making
places
relaxing

**Update your space
with more plants!
USM makes it possible.**
usm.com

Visit our authorized sales partners or our USM Showrooms
in Bern, Hamburg, London, Munich, New York, Paris, Tokyo

Coutts

That doesn't mean a suit and tie – unless that's your style. It means doing things your way, reflecting your individuality and spirit. Like bespoke wealth management at Coutts that's tailored to your personal needs and ambitions.

REAL SUCCESS TAKES TRUE CHARACTER

Certified

Corporation

ANDREW TUCK ON FINDING THE CONFIDENCE TO DREAM A LITTLE BIGGER

There's an invisible barrier that too often deters people who could be running their own enterprise from taking the leap. It's the belief that entrepreneurs are somehow a different creature to everyone else; that they all share the same traits; that they were born with this propensity already wired into their brains. The notion seems to be that if at heart you are not a bit brutal, a mean dealmaker, you will never make it. That's rubbish and, what's more, this type of thinking deters lots of men and women from realising their dreams. The skills that you need to endure the hardships of going it alone or of taking over a family enterprise and making it flourish again can be learnt on the job, absorbed by surrounding yourself with wise mentors – or, to be blunt, paying for a business coach.

Every year as we put together this handbook for entrepreneurs, I am struck by the incredible personal stories and sheer determination of the people who end up on the pages and wonder how we could entice more people to join them. So that's why this time we asked three of our writers to check in with a business coach to see how they would springboard them into action (though, to be clear, I am hoping that for now they stay writing for MONOCLE). Coaching is a field where you can spend a lot of money and see few results but hopefully the story (*page 50*) will show how – chosen wisely – a good coach will make you focus, shape your ideas and get you to step up to the plate.

And, this being MONOCLE where the notion of quality of life always matters, we have also tried to show you how being a successful business owner can also happen in, say, bucolic Estonia (it's a perfect place to hone a food enterprise) or in a city with a gentler pace such as Catania or Guadalajara (and the extra hours of sunshine and light can also soothe at the close of a stressful day).

And, to keep things challenging, we have also tracked down people who have ignored the common advice to do one thing well and instead decided to run *two* enterprises well – and in doing so have often discovered interesting synchronicities between their various company offspring. Read our report (*page 86*) to learn why running a wine business helps your fashion company or having an architecture practice makes you potential restaurateurs too.

In this inspiring issue we also wanted to celebrate the perks of work – how company owners can make their offices more welcoming and joyful but also just how being together as teams can be empowering. In our Expo (*page 115*) we have found companies that understand how to make going to work feel special – from time off when you become a puppy parent to the chance to do some gardening in your lunchtime and from an office sauna to a company bar. Perhaps that's another potential sign of a good entrepreneur: a willingness to mix things up and know when *not* to work too. And then there's our story on diaspora business communities in Africa (*page 76*): Moroccans trading in Côte d'Ivoire to French viticulturalists in South Africa. Another group of people who became successful entrepreneurs for a range of very different reasons – and sometimes just out of necessity.

So as you read our reports, remember that you too could be on these pages. Starting or growing an existing company needs lots of skills but remember that they can all be absorbed along the way. Don't put off being a success. Good luck. — Ⓜ

If you have ideas, thoughts or feedback, please feel free to contact me at at@monocle.com.

The
ENTREPRENEURS

CONTENTS.

Slow-down destinations. *Catania, page 054 — 065*

'How-to' interviews. *Doutor, page 038 — 047*

Two companies. *Joey Wölffer, page 086 — 089*

Culture. *Sleeping with the past, page 091 — 101*

The ENTREPRENEURS

Baltic revival. *Southern Estonia, page 108 — 113*

TRAVEL & HOSPITALITY

EXPO

PLUS

Back to basics. *Basicnet, page 104 — 107*

Expo. *Perks of the job, page 115 — 130*

KEY TO WRITERS

(CAG) Carolina Abbott Galvão. (DBA) Désirée Bandli. (AMB) Ann Binlot. (PBU) Petri Burtsoff. (ABC) Annabelle Chapman. (MCH) Melkon Charchoglyan. (GCH) Grace Charlton. (JAF) Josh Fehnert. (AMG) Ann Marie Gardner. (EH) Erin Hale. (NAH) Noor Amylia Hilda. (MLH) Mina Holland. (JIR) Jessica Iredale. (DK) Daphne Karnezis. (JSK) Jeyup S Kwaak. (TLE) Tomos Lewis. (TLW) Tara Loader Wilkinson. (CL) Christopher Lord. (NM) Nic Monisse. (CHR) Chiara Rimella. (SRO) Stella Roos. (LR) Laura Rysman. (GRS) Gregory Scruggs. (ASE) Alexis Self. (NT) Natalie Theodosi. (FW) Fiona Wilson. (NXE) Naomi Xu Elegant.

COVER ILLUSTRATION:
Tommy Parker

Because you give your dreams the love you deserve.
Experience now the drēmər® bed at your nearest Hästens store.
HASTENS.COM

Hästens
since 1852

ⓂⓇ MONOCLE 24

A SMART SOUNDTRACK THAT IS JUST THE BUSINESS – EVERY DAY OF THE WEEK

For over 10 years, Monocle 24 has been broadcasting about the best in entrepreneurship, commerce and more.

35 weekly premieres
15 original news shows every week
1 million-plus listens every month

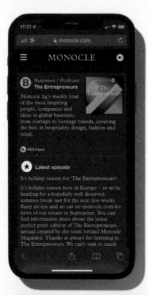

Up to date...
Listen live and stay in the moment.

...or up to you
Download your favourite shows at any time.

Total coverage
In business, culture, design, media and news.

MONOCLE 24
Unrivalled radio and perfect podcasts

See the schedule at *monocle.com/ radio* or listen via Apple Podcasts, Spotify or wherever you get your audio.

In good company

THE GLOBALIST
Leading lights

Stay on top of the international news agenda with our flagship current affairs and business show, which features a smart review of the latest front pages. Reporting that matters, wherever you are in the world.

THE MONOCLE DAILY
Top stories

Hear Monocle 24's take on the news, with sharp reporting and analysis from our global network.

THE ENTREPRENEURS
Good ideas

A weekly tour of the most inspiring people, companies and views in global business.

KONFEKT KORNER:
THE PODCAST

THE BULLETIN WITH UBS
Fresh thinking

Fine minds offer savvy insights into the places, products and people shaping the week ahead.

KONFEKT KORNER
Well turned out

Lively conversation and canny reports about fashion, interiors, craft, food and travel.

Shake your money maker!

Bergos. Shook.

BERGOS
HUMAN PRIVATE BANKING

Since 1590 and/or 2021

MAGAZINE. RADIO.
ONLINE. FILM.

EDITORIAL

Tyler Brûlé. Editorial Director & Chairman… *tb@monocle.com*
Andrew Tuck. Editor in Chief… *at@monocle.com*
Richard Spencer Powell. Creative Director… *rsp@monocle.com*
Josh Fehnert. Editor… *jaf@monocle.com*
Jacqueline Deacon. Production Director… *jd@monocle.com*
Lewis Huxley. Chief Sub Editor… *lh@monocle.com*
Matthew Beaman. Photography Director… *mpb@monocle.com*
Nolan Giles. Executive Editor… *nsg@monocle.com*
Chiara Rimella. Culture Editor… *chr@monocle.com*
David Hodari. Business Editor… *dho@monocle.com*
Natalie Theodosi. Fashion Editor… *nt@monocle.com*
Nic Monisse. Deputy Design Editor… *nm@monocle.com*
Alexis Self. Associate Editor… *as@monocle.com*
Marcela Palek. Style Director… *mp@monocle.com*
Daphné Hézard. Fashion Director (Paris)… *dhz@monocle.com*
Robert Bound. Senior Correspondent… *rb@monocle.com*
Sophie Grove. Senior Correspondent… *sgr@monocle.com*
Kyoko Tamoto. Fashion Markets Editor… *kt@monocle.com*
Carolina Abbott Galvão. Researcher… *cag@monocle.com*
Grace Charlton. Researcher… *gch@monocle.com*
Jack Simpson. Editorial Assistant… *jms@monocle.com*

DESIGN

Sam Brogan. Art Director… *sbr@monocle.com*
Alex Milnes. Photography Editor… *ami@monocle.com*
Jessica North-Lewis. Designer… *jnl@monocle.com*
Amara Eno. Assistant Photography Editor… *ae@monocle.com*
Oli Kellar. Junior Designer… *ok@monocle.com*
Kamila Lozinska. Junior Photography Editor… *kl@monocle.com*

BUREAUX

Fiona Wilson. Bureau Chief & Senior Asia Editor (TOKYO)… *fw@monocle.com*
Junichi Toyofuku. Associate Bureau Chief (TOKYO)… *jt@monocle.com*
James Chambers. Bureau Chief & Asia Editor (HONG KONG)… *jch@monocle.com*
Naomi Xu Elegant. Writer/Researcher (HONG KONG)… *nxe@monocle.com*
Ed Stocker. Europe Editor at Large (MILAN)… *ejs@monocle.com*
Christopher Lord. US Editor (LOS ANGELES)… *cl@monocle.com*
Carlo Silberschmidt. Production Co-ordinator (ZÜRICH)… *cs@monocle.com*

SUB EDITING

Yo Zushi. Senior Sub Editor… *yz@monocle.com*
Sarah Cohen. Sub Editor … *sco@monocle.com*
Sonia Zhuravlyova. Sub Editor… *sz@monocle.com*

ONLINE

Rogerio Mota. Senior Digital Designer… *rmm@monocle.com*
Juan Muñoz. Senior Web Developer… *jmh@monocle.com*
Valentina Labib. Web Developer… *vb@monocle.com*
Bill Whitehouse. Digital Content Manager… *bw@monocle.com*
Emilie Wade. Assistant Digital Content Producer… *ew@monocle.com*

BOOKS

Joe Pickard. Head of Book Publishing… *jp@monocle.com*
Molly Price. Deputy Editor, Book Publishing… *mpr@monocle.com*
Amy Van Den Berg. Assistant Editor, Book Publishing… *av@monocle.com*
Sarah Kramer. Production Manager, Book Publishing… *sk@monocle.com*

FILM

Megan Revell. Senior Producer… *mr@monocle.com*

MONOCLE 24 RADIO

Tom Edwards. Head of Radio… *te@monocle.com*
Markus Hippi. Senior Producer/Presenter… *mh@monocle.com*
Rhys James. Senior News Producer… *rj@monocle.com*
Carlota Rebelo. Producer/Presenter… *cr@monocle.com*
Fernando Augusto Pacheco. Producer & Senior Correspondent… *fp@monocle.com*
Emma Searle. Producer… *es@monocle.com*
Sophie Monaghan-Coombs Associate Producer… *smc@monocle.com*
Lilian Fawcett Researcher… *ljf@monocle.com*
Désirée Bandli Researcher… *dfb@monocle.com*
Sam Impey. Head of Production… *sji@monocle.com*
David Stevens. Senior Studio Manager… *djs@monocle.com*
Christy Evans. Studio Manager… *ce@monocle.com*
Mae-Li Evans. Studio Manager… *me@monocle.com*
Nora Hoel. Studio Manager… *nh@monocle.com*
Steph Chungu. Studio Manager… *sc@monocle.com*
Callum Mclean. Studio Manager… *cm@monocle.com*
Adam Heaton. Studio Manager… *ah@monocle.com*
Jack Jewers. Sound Editor… *jj@monocle.com*

CORRESPONDENTS

Liam Aldous. (MADRID)… *la@monocle.com*
Aarti Betigeri. (CANBERRA)… *aab@monocle.com*
Lars Bevanger. (OSLO)… *lab@monocle.com*
Michael Booth. (COPENHAGEN)… *mb@monocle.com*
Kimberly Bradley. (BERLIN)… *kab@monocle.com*
Petri Burtsoff. (HELSINKI)… *pbu@monocle.com*
Ivan Carvalho. (MILAN)… *ic@monocle.com*
Annabelle Chapman. (WARSAW)… *abc@monocle.com*
Guy De Launey. (LJUBLJANA)… *gdl@monocle.com*
Zach Dundas. (PORTLAND, OREGON)… *zd@monocle.com*
Lucinda Elliott. (LATIN AMERICA AFFAIRS)… *le@monocle.com*
Mary Fitzgerald. (NORTH AFRICA)… *mfi@monocle.com*
Mary Holland. (NEW YORK)… *mho@monocle.com*
Sasha Issenberg. (US POLITICAL CORRESPONDENT)… *si@monocle.com*
Daphne Karnezis. (ATHENS)… *dk@monocle.com*
Alexei Korolyov. (VIENNA, RADIO)… *ako@monocle.com*
Jeyup S Kwaak. (SEOUL)… *jsk@monocle.com*
Gabriel Leigh. (TRANSPORT)… *gl@monocle.com*
Tomos Lewis. (TORONTO)… *tle@monocle.com*
Liv Lewitschnik. (STOCKHOLM)… *ll@monocle.com*
Gaia Lutz. (LISBON)… *gsl@monocle.com*
Charlotte McDonald-Gibson. (BRUSSELS)… *cmg@monocle.com*
Leila Molana-Allen. (BEIRUT)… *lmo@monocle.com*
Anastasia Moloney. (BOGOTÁ)… *anm@monocle.com*
David Phelan. (TECHNOLOGY)… *dwp@monocle.com*
David Plaisant. (ROME)… *dmp@monocle.com*
Lyndee Prickitt. (NEW DELHI)… *llp@monocle.com*
Henry Rees-Sheridan. (NEW YORK, RADIO)… *hrs@monocle.com*
Gwen Robinson. (BANGKOK)… *gr@monocle.com*
Sarah Rowland. (SOUTHERN STATES, USA)… *sr@monocle.com*
Laura Rysman. (CENTRAL ITALY)… *lr@monocle.com*
Janek Schmidt. (MUNICH)… *js@monocle.com*
Hannah Lucinda Smith. (ISTANBUL)… *hls@monocle.com*
Olga Tokariuk. (UKRAINE)… *ot@monocle.com*
Annick Weber. (LUXEMBOURG)… *aw@monocle.com*
Benno Zogg. (SECURITY)… *bz@monocle.com*

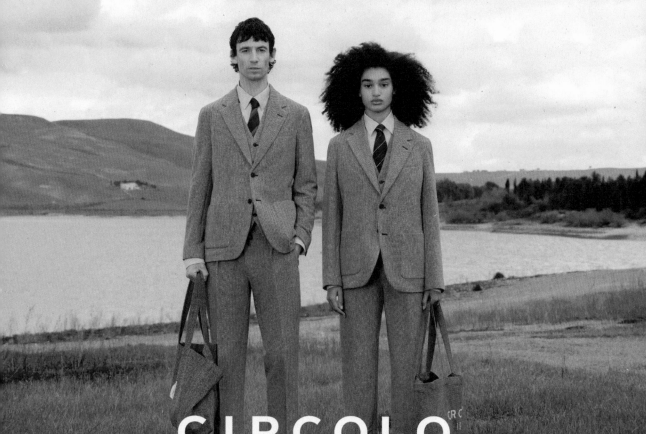

CIRCOLO

1901

PUBLISHING. MARKETING. DISTRIBUTION. RETAIL.

PUBLISHING
Anders Braso. Publisher… *ab@monocle.com*

ADVERTISING
Luke Courtier. Associate Publisher… *lc@monocle.com*
Guido de Boer. Advertising Director – Asia… *gb@monocle.com*
Antje Petzold. Advertising Manager – Europe… *anp@monocle.com*
Chester Bentley. Intern

CREATIVE SOLUTIONS
Kate Parkinson. Creative Solutions Director… *kp@monocle.com*
Niall Flynn. Global Partnerships Editor… *nf@monocle.com*
Emma Croft. Creative Solutions Project Manager… *ec@monocle.com*

ADVERTISING OFFICES
MIA. Milan (ITALY)… *mia@miasrl.it*
Nartnittha Jirarayapong. Bangkok (THAILAND)… *noo@njintermedia.com*
Keith Lee. Taipei (TAIWAN)… *leekh@ms4.hinet.net*
Seo Jin-Mahn. Seoul (SOUTH KOREA)… *jinmahnseo@doobee.com*
Sam Jones. USA… *swj@monocle.com*

CIRCULATION AND SUBSCRIPTIONS
Holly Anderson. Circulation & Brand Partnerships Director… *han@monocle.com*
Madison Cilluffo. Intern

RETAIL
Philippa Cooper. Head of Retail & Hospitality… *pc@monocle.com*
Raffael Lienert. Senior Operations Manager for Retail & Hospitality… *rl@monocle.com*
Rosie Croft. E-Commerce & Merchandising Manager… *rc@monocle.com*
Mathilde Felter. Supply-Chain & Logistics Manager… *maf@monocle.com*
Diego Lopez De La Fuente. Product Development Manager… *dl@monocle.com*
Eleonora Frattini. Retail Creative & Merchandising Assistant… *ef@monocle.com*

CUSTOMER SERVICE
Lina Constanza Mendez Saenz. Director of Customer Experience… *lcms@monocle.com*
Benson Batty. Customer Relations & Insights Executive… *bb@monocle.com*
Jenny Lam. Customer Relations Assistant… *jla@monocle.com*

FINANCE
Anna Nunziata. Chief Operating Officer… *an@monocle.com*
Pauline Ho. Group Treasurer… *pho@monocle.com*
Taj Singh. Finance Director… *ts@monocle.com*
Joe Shafi. Finance Manager… *jsh@monocle.com*
Farzana Ali. Commercial Accountant… *fa@monocle.com*
Kiran Ladwa. Credit Controller… *kla@monocle.com*
Danica Fernandes. Management Accountant… *df@monocle.com*
Naomi Lamptey. Accounts Payable Assistant… *nla@monocle.com*

THE BOARD
Richard Atkinson, Tyler Brûlé. Directors
Tyler Brûlé. Chairman

EVENTS
Hannah Grundy. Head of Brand, Communications & Events… *hg@monocle.com*

EDITORIAL DIRECTOR'S SUPPORT
Izumi Dresen. Executive Assistant… *id@monocle.com*

HEAD OFFICE
Monocle
Midori House
1 Dorset Street
London W1U 4EG
TEL: +44 (0)20 7725 4388
info@monocle.com
customerservice@monocle.com

FRONT OF HOUSE
Brenda Tuohy.
bt@monocle.com

ZÜRICH HQ & BUREAUX
Toronto
776 College Street
Toronto, ON M6G 1C6
TEL: +1 647 694 2626

Tokyo
1F, Luna Rossa
1-19-2 Tomigaya
Shibuya-ku, Tokyo 151-0063
TEL: +81 (0)3 6407 0350

Hong Kong
Shop 1, Bo Fung Mansion
1–4 St Francis Yard
Wan Chai, Hong Kong
TEL: +852 2804 2626

Zürich
90 Dufourstrasse
CH-8008, Zürich
TEL: +41 44 368 7001

Los Angeles
Platform, Unit 105,
8820 Washington Boulevard,
Culver City, Los Angeles
TEL: +1 310 982 2966

SHOPS
London
18 Chiltern Street, London W1U 7QA
TEL: +44 (0)20 7486 8770
londonshop@monocle.com
Sam Langley: *sla@monocle.com*

Hong Kong
Shop 1, Bo Fung Mansion, 1–4 St Francis Yard, Wan Chai, Hong Kong
TEL: +852 2804 2626
hkshop@monocle.com
Harry CK Wong: *hw@monocle.com*

Toronto
776 College Street
Toronto, ON M6G 1C6
TEL: +1 647 694 2626
torontoshop@monocle.com
Catalina Posada: *cp@monocle.com*

Tokyo
1F, Luna Rossa, 1-19-2 Tomigaya
Shibuya-ku, Tokyo, 151-0063
TEL: +81 (0)3 6407 0845
tokyoshop@monocle.com
Nanako Sato: *nas@monocle.com*

Merano
25 Via Dante, 39012, Merano
meranoshopshop@monocle.com
Linda Egger: *ge@monocle.com*

Zürich
90 Dufourstrasse, CH-8008, Zürich
TEL: +41 44 368 7001
zurichshop@monocle.com
Raffael Lienert: *rl@monocle.com*

Los Angeles
Platform, 8820 Washington
Boulevard, Culver City, Los Angeles
TEL: +1 310 982 2966
lashop@monocle.com
Sam Jones: *swj@monocle.com*

TRAVEL RETAIL
Hong Kong
Hong Kong International Airport,
Gate 61, Terminal 1
TEL: +852 2116 5530
Harry CK Wong: *hw@monocle.com*

MONOCLE CAFÉS
London
18 Chiltern Street, London W1U 7QA
TEL: +44 (0)20 7135 2040

Zürich
90 Dufourstrasse, CH-8008, Zürich
TEL: +41 44 368 7001

KIOSK
Zürich
Jelmoli, Seidengasse 1, 8001 Zürich
Samuele De Santis: *sds@monocle.com*

CONTRIBUTORS.

This bumper handbook of entrepreneurial insight, inspiration and advice is very much a collaborative effort. We tasked our global network of writers, photographers and illustrators to find, report on and present the world's most dynamic business leaders and companies that our readers would be wise to draw knowledge from. Inevitably, in the process, they accrued some lessons of their own. Here, a few of them expand on what they took from working on this edition of *The Entrepreneurs* and outline their personal career journeys.

Our newly minted Seoul correspondent, **Jeyup S Kwaak**, sat down for a session with South Korean executive trainer Kim Byung-heon as part of our feature exploring *whether business coaching really works, on page 50*. Initially he felt awkward but, "It became easier by the minute to own my strengths and weaknesses as I began to verbalise them to a receptive audience," he says. Kwaak also had the revelation that "CEOs are human too". "They have the same doubts and fears as all of us," he says. "That makes former executives great sounding boards for aspiring entrepreneurs."

Kwaak started his career at *The Korea Times*. After a two-year mandatory military service, he held staff reporter jobs at that paper and *The Wall Street Journal*. Since then he has worked as an independent journalist covering all things Korean and East Asian, from diplomatic relations to South Korea's burgeoning entertainment sector.

A recent addition to our crack squad of journalists is New York-based fashion writer and editor **Jessica Iredale**. She spoke to Libby Wadle, CEO of classic American clothing brand J Crew, for our *'how-to' interviews, which start on page 38*. During the discussion, Iredale discovered that she and Wadle both studied at Boston College and that "women are giving up their skinny jeans in favour of wider-leg styles more easily than you might think".

Iredale worked at *Women's Wear Daily* for almost 15 years and says, "I was incredibly lucky to have two amazing mentors, Bridget Foley and Etta Froio, who are proper fashion journalists, the likes of which are simply not made any more." Now she contributes to *The New York Times*, *Town & Country* and other publications.

In our *essays section, which starts on page 68*, seven savvy writers muse on subjects as diverse as how hostage-negotiator skills can help leaders and the importance of taking a lunch break. Uniting these ideas with bright washes of colour is the artwork of Milanese illustrator **Giordano Poloni**. Bringing to life the essays gave Poloni some pointers on better ways to manage his time, sell his work and deal with clients. "I don't see myself as a businessman but being a freelance artist is like being one on my own," he says. Poloni began his career as an illustrator late: he only started drawing when he was 30. "I was working as an editor and VFX artist but I was not satisfied," he says. "So I followed my passion and tried to make illustration my main work – and I did it." He has an ambition to work for his favourite publication, *The New Yorker*, but he'd also love to design film posters and book jackets.

Nairobi-based journalist **Naveena Kottoor** wrote our illuminating article about *entrepreneurial diasporas in Africa on page 76*. She took away three fascinating insights from the experience. "While angst and gloom dominate the mood in Europe and the US, there is a real sense that the glass is half full among entrepreneurs in Africa," she says. "Also, I was perplexed to find French entrepreneurs traumatised by the thought of running a business in France," she adds. "The paperwork and taxes there seem to be insurmountable impediments." And finally, Kottoor observes, "When life gives them lemons, Iranians make lemonade and excel at it."

Kottoor's career has taken her all over the world. She started in Berlin, working for National Public Radio and the BBC, then moved with the corporation to London. "I felt really energised by the city and ended up staying longer than I had thought," she says. In 2013 she relocated to Tunis, where she reported on the green shoots of the Arab spring. Since then she's lived in Brussels, Beirut and Berlin again, before settling in Nairobi in 2021.

These correspondents are only a few of the many talented people involved in putting together this issue of *The Entrepreneurs*. Turn the page to enjoy and be enlightened by their words and pictures. — Ⓜ

The
ENTREPRENEURS

SUNSPEL

ENGLAND 1860

LUXURY BRITISH ESSENTIALS SINCE

SUNSPEL.COM

Thank you so very much for the beer. It's as
delicious as you said, so much so that I am
struggling to share it.

I look forward to drinking one with you.

Joe Trivelli - The River Cafe

willsark.com

ALL THE RIGHT MOVES

We profile founders and firms that have nimbly switched direction or grasped novel ideas and tapped new markets. Plus, the reads that you never knew you needed and hot tips from top CEOs.

Go full circle
Meet the businesses cutting waste and ramping up reuse in the circular economy. We learn about the Londoners turning the tables on the old ways of doing things, and making both healthy profits and attractive products along the way.
See page 30.

Get out more
Seattle-based bike and ski-maker Evo knows how to get close to its customers. The retailer is building itself an impressive property portfolio, recently finishing a housing development with homes and more for fans of the brand.
See page 31.

Turn the page
When it comes to the business of the business book, most titles can be a tad tedious. Our solution? We've taken a tongue-in-cheek look at the entrepreneurial tomes we'd like to see written and the notable niches we'd gladly read about.
See page 34.

Home win
A Swiss entrepreneur sharing his process and netting a winner

The training programmes of leading professional athletic clubs (think football, hockey and basketball teams) are often kept top secret to give them a winning edge. Despite this highly competitive sporting market, Hans-Peter Strebel, a Swiss pharmaceutical entrepreneur and president of ice hockey club Eissportverein Zug (EVZ), is sharing his secrets to success with competitors, solo professional athletes and teams competing in events that lack the financial pull of more lucrative sports.

How? Well, through OYM – short for On Your Marks – in Zug, Switzerland. Its facility an hour from Zürich enables Swiss athletes and teams to access high-end training. Strebel's initial plans for the centre that has since become OYM was to create a training base for EVZ but the idea evolved to include other professional and semi-professional athletes. "I originally wanted to enable young players at EVZ to have continuous development, from juniors to the top level," says Strebel. "But as we were visiting several sports-training centres in Switzerland and abroad [as part of the research for the enterprise], we realised that we wanted to help elite athletes in general."

In its short life since launching in 2020, OYM's clients have included the Swiss women's handball team (which, prior to OYM opening, was faced with the decision to professionalise or fold) and bobsleigh pilot Michael Vogt.

To tap into the benefits of OYM, individuals and teams need to have a Swiss Olympic Card (meaning that they are close to the qualification requirements for entry to the Games) and be willing to pay between €25,000 and €35,000 for a year. And while the price might sound steep, the benefits are significant. OYM members are given access to chefs who oversee nutrition plans, physiotherapists and rehabilitation experts. There's also an ice rink, athletics hall, gym, stair ramps, a sprint track and "turf" area, where the athletes train and are coached by the centre's performance directors,

1   2

who meticulously track every aspect of the sessions.

"Normally, when athletes and teams are training, they'll do a detailed test every three to five months," says OYM's Andrin Studerus, who takes MONOCLE on a tour of the facility. "But between those tests, it's hard to know how you're progressing. This approach means that every training session delivers data, which can ensure that the athletes are on the right track."

It's a point of difference that Strebel is keen to stress. "Anyone could build the training infrastructure," he says. "But the fact that there are scientists here who are involved in developing solutions tailored to individual athletes is unique."

This, he says, is what sets OYM apart, and why there's interest for the model to be replicated abroad. Though tight-lipped on the subject, the OYM team says that there are ongoing discussions with overseas investors keen to franchise the concept. It's high praise for any business venture – after all, imitation (or franchising) is the highest form of flattery. — NM

> "Having scientists here developing solutions tailored to individual athletes is something unique"

1.
Multiuse court at OYM
2.
On your marks...
3.
Winners take the stairs

Toolkit takeaway
Kept private, OYM could have given the founder's hockey team a competitive edge. But opening up the concept to other athletes and potential competitors paved the way for more income to be reinvested.

Pivot pioneers
Global

When new opportunities present themselves, entrepreneurs must weigh up their options: curb their enthusiasm or take a chance? For these five companies, a change in trajectory ended up making their fortunes. — GCH

 Tiffany & Co
USA
The iconic US jeweller started as a stationery shop and fine goods emporium in 1837 in New York. The first day's sales total: $4.98. It wasn't until the 1860s that the company changed tack and hit its stride, focusing on gold jewellery and making luxury available to Americans. Its operating income in 2021: $900m (€796m).

 Nintendo
Japan
Back in 1889, Nintendo was a humble playing-cards manufacturer before it shuffled the deck. When the world of electronics opened up new entertainment possibilities in the 1960s, Nintendo acted quickly after a string of failed ventures and diminishing sales. The firm introduced Magnavox Odyssey, one of the first major games consoles, in 1972 and last year pulled in €4.6bn.

 Lamborghini
Italy
Engineer Ferruccio Lamborghini started off making tractors for his father (and later for family friends) to use in rebuilding postwar Italy's agriculture. As his designs evolved in the early 1960s, his focus shifted to cars. Today, the renowned marque makes €1.95bn a year.

 Play-Doh
USA
Play-Doh was first sold in the 1930s as a cleaning agent that could remove coal residue from wallpaper. As oil and gas furnaces became more popular in the 1950s, demand dropped and the firm struggled until the Cincinnati-based owners heard about a teacher using the clay in arts and crafts classes. The addition of colours created a wildly popular putty.

 Peugeot
France
The Sochaux-based car-maker started out in 1810 as a manufacturer of coffee grinders and steel components, such as umbrella frames. By the end of the 19th century, however, the firm was applying its knowledge of grinding gears to engines. Peugeot's latest financial report confirmed a turnover of €23.9bn.

Toolkit takeaway
These five firms should remind even the most surefooted CEO to roll with the market and grab opportunities. Stay nimble and open-minded, especially if that involves a leap from souped-up tractors to supercars.

Monuments to industry
Global

Some small towns owe their existence to an industry and locals are only too proud to celebrate it. Others, however, are beholden to the firms that helped to form them. This can reveal itself in several ways, from annual parades to the name of a place. Alumínio in Brazil, Tabaco in the Philippines or Gas in the US state of Kansas (we're assuming it's the fuel variety) are leaders in this regard. Other towns, however, build artworks dedicated to their industries; it's a celebratory approach that offers an extraordinary visual reminder of what keeps the towns ticking. With this in mind, here are five of our favourite monuments to trades that have shaped their towns. — NM

Duravit Toilet
Germany

Duravit is a leading manufacturer of designer bathrooms. It has called the Black Forest home since 1817 and gives back to the region through various projects, such as the installation of state-of-the-art public toilets in the town of Titisee. Our favourite of its contributions, though, is a 12 metre-high loo that it created in Hornberg, designed by Philippe Starck. Visitors can climb to the top and enjoy sweeping vistas. How's that for a perch with a view?

National Trout Memorial
USA

Commercial, recreational and tribal fisheries on the US Great Lakes are collectively valued at more than $7bn (€7bn) annually in turnover and support more than 75,000 jobs. Many towns claim to be the heart of this industry but Kalkaska, Michigan, secured that status by playing host to the National Trout Festival and building the National Trout Memorial – a 5-metre-long trout that appears to be leaping from a pond in the town centre.

Evolution of Textile
Tunisia

Ksar Hellal is dubbed Tunisia's textile capital. To assert this status, artist Abdelfattah Boussetta was commissioned to design and make a sculpture that represented a moving piece of cloth. Completed in 1997, the work is topped with a dove that Boussetta says represents the forward movement of the industry in Ksar Hellal and the creativity of the sector.

Udine Chair
Italy

For years, a 20 metre-high chair stood on a roundabout in the tiny Friuli town of Manzano. The area is home to many high-end furniture manufacturers, including Mattiazzi and Calligaris, and the piece was meant to symbolise the significance of the region, appropriately dubbed the "chair triangle". Sadly, a lack of maintenance meant the seat had to be dismantled – a reminder that even furniture made in a region renowned for its quality needs care.

Fork of Vevey
Switzerland

The village of Vevey, on the shores of Lake Geneva, shares a proud association with food giant Nestlé. The company's HQ is here, as is Alimentarium, a food museum with a permanent Nestlé exhibition. As though this were not enough of a celebration, an eight metre-high fork has been installed in the lake itself, as a physical marker of the town and its industry.

Toolkit takeaway

Investing in a town can take many forms – celebrating local businesses with artistic installations can help to put them on the map. But be sure to look after your community before building an idol to your industry.

Iranian-American Roxanne Varza is the director of Station F, the world's largest start-up campus. Based in Paris, the incubator has helped to raise €1.8bn in funding since it launched in 2015, with nearly €500m in the first half of 2022 alone. Varza shares some advice for founders. — GCH

1.
"I encourage entrepreneurs to think about the 'why' of their business. There's so much hype around having your own company that some people just do it because they think it's cool."

2.
"Running a business is hard. You don't often read about the difficulties (though now, with the economic climate, maybe you do). You don't see the struggles, especially in the early years, which is what we see at Station F. Ask yourself if you're ready for a marathon."

3.
"Think about why you are the right person for that business: what sets you apart? What makes you special?"

Clean bean
A coffee roaster becomes Kenya's hot new thing

In 2018, while casting around for a new venture following the sale of his Nairobi-based pizza business, Ritesh Doshi would walk his dogs from his home in the Kenyan capital to a local café, Spring Valley Coffee.

"They served the best coffee in town and were dog-friendly so it became a daily ritual," says the former investment banker and LSE graduate. And when the owners wanted to sell, Doshi bought the business. "I knew nothing about coffee except that it was a growing market," he says.

With a view to slowly expanding, Doshi began looking for farmers to buy beans from beyond the ones that Spring Valley Coffee was working with at the time of acquisition. It was a tough task: in an industry with a questionable track record on working conditions and environmental damage, sourcing beans responsibly was a challenge. But Doshi

rose to it – and then went further. He has partnered with seven co-operative and small producers, pays a premium – sometimes 15 per cent above the going rate – and helps in other ways (he's built wash stations for female farmers).

It's a move that has resonated with wholesalers and customers: Spring Valley Coffee can now be sipped in 150 locations across Kenya and has seven of its own cafés. Doshi's approach is a reminder that growth doesn't have to come at the expense of quality or responsible production. "Business has to be about more than just profit," he says. "It has to have purpose too." — TLW

Toolkit takeaway
Wake up and smell the coffee: a business that demonstrates that it is investing in quality and responsibly sourced products can appeal to savvy customers and clients, making for a loyal following and a mean cup of joe.

> "Spring Valley Coffee's approach has resonated with wholesalers and customers, and it can now be sipped in 150 locations"

Danish renaissance
Reviving the family firm

Continuing the legacy of a family firm is challenging after the founders have moved on. It's a situation faced by the families behind Hvidt & Mølgaard Furniture.

The Copenhagen-based company was started and run by Peter Hvidt and Orla Mølgaard-Nielsen between 1944 and 1975. Now it is experiencing a rebirth led by the founders' families and their grandchildren, Kasper Mølgaard and Malene Hvidt (*pictured*).

"It's different from setting up a new company because it's in the framework of our heritage and the designs that already exist," says Mølgaard. It's a sentiment that Hvidt agrees with when we meet the duo just prior to the reissue of Hvidt & Mølgaard's iconic X Chair, the seat's first commercial production in decades. "They created everlasting designs so we didn't feel that we had to go in and reshape or modernise our heritage," she says.

The families began working on the revival in 2016, delving into the company's archive. "What was really important was making long-lasting furniture. If you look at the originals, they are still functioning today," says Mølgaard. They eventually entered into an arrangement with Danish furniture maker &Tradition, which produces the new pieces.

It's an impressive turnaround for a company that was dormant for decades. It's also a reminder that when reviving a heritage business, it's worth recreating the original hits. "We didn't restart Hvidt & Mølgaard for the money," says Mølgaard. "We just wanted people to experience how great the furniture is." — NM

Toolkit takeaway
Whether you're reviving a family restaurant or storied furniture brand, breathing new life into old favourites – be it a classic recipe or a renowned chair – can be smart route to renewed success.

1

2

4

5

Virtuous circle
*Why saving your neighbour's
waste is good business*

With the afternoon sun shining on the newly refurbished warehouse buildings of Hackney Wick, the long-overlooked London neighbourhood could pass for a buzzy corner of Sydney or Brooklyn. "There are so many nooks to explore," says Marta Zabik from urban planning studio Tapestry, who's on hand to take us on a tour of the businesses involved in a new circular-high-street programme. The concept, Zabik says, is straightforward: champion companies in the area that are working towards a closed-loop system by limiting single-use items, sharing resources or by re-purposing waste from neighbourhood businesses to make new products. "The idea is to help people discover the sustainable businesses that are already closing the loop."

The initiative is supported by the Hackney Wick Fish Island Community Development Trust and Tapestry, which facilitate connections between the enterprises involved. It is helping to shape Hackney Wick as a hub of ecological innovation, with that ever-elusive sociopolitical goal of creating a sense of community.

For proof of concept, Zabik points to Refill Therapy, a zero-waste shop

3

"If we can show
that a closed-
loop system can
be both
lucrative and
create beautiful
products,
that's a
game-changer"

PHOTOGRAPHERS: AMARA ENO, BEN LINDBLOOM

founded in 2021. Here manager Sebastien Gherghel explains that a range of its products – dog treats, for example – has been made from oats discarded during the beer-making process at the nearby East London Brewery. "We have so many connections with the other smaller companies in the area," says Gherghel. Another business with similar connections is restaurant Silo, which has partnered with a potter who turns its leftover glass vessels into sleek ceramics.

Founded by chef Douglas McMaster, Silo sources its produce directly from foragers, farmers and fishermen who limit waste with reusable containers, such as old-fashioned milk and cream pails. Through a resourceful approach to cooking, 95 per cent of the food ends up on diners' plates with the remainder sent to compost. "It becomes an obsession – you can't unsee waste," says McMaster. This led him to contact Maltese potter Mark Ciavola, who moved his Potter's Thumb studio into the restaurant's canalside location in 2021. Here, Ciavola repurposes Silo's used bottles into clay, a process with a patent pending.

"There's so much discarded glass, it's important to create this blueprint," says Ciavola. The result speaks for itself: earthy green and cool-grey tiles and plates that retain a glassy sheen are used throughout Silo. "If we can demonstrate that a closed-loop system can be both financially lucrative and create beautiful products, that's a game-changer," says McMaster. "We're trying to achieve excellence here. We need to work harder than other restaurants to prove that an environmentally focused, circular business doesn't have to compromise."

Here's hoping that Silo, Potter's Thumb and the likes of Refill Therapy's ongoing success can help make the point. And, in the process, inspire other neighbourhoods to follow suit. — GCH

Toolkit takeaway
By rallying together, businesses can create a circular economy that reduces waste and overheads. A happy by-product? When businesses work hand-in-hand, community bonds are strengthened too.

1.
Silo restaurant
2.
Marta Zabik of Tapestry studio
3.
Sebastien Gherghel of Refill Therapy
4.
Plate made from glass bottles
5.
Dog treats
6.
On the menu

Moving mountains
An uphill battle to build a neighbourhood around a business

In Snoqualmie Pass, a mountain town an hour's drive east of Seattle in the Cascade mountains, a steady stream of hikers and mountain bikers are returning from alpine tracks. On this sunny morning they enter a renovated century-old firehouse that's home to a café, a grocer and a co-working space, part of a new mixed-use neighbourhood called The Pass Life.

Several greet Bryce Phillips (*pictured*) as he eats breakfast on the café terrace. A former professional skier, Phillips is the founder and CEO of Evo, an outdoor-equipment retailer that has grown over 20 years to now include bricks-and-mortar properties covering outdoor recreation, retail, hospitality, travel and culture.

"Evo is really an outdoor-experience business," says Phillips. "Retail is still the primary economic driver but we're looking to deliver a suite of experiences globally that are unlike anything else. If you have a passion to get outside, then we want to physically be there with you."

It's no surprise that the morning crowd greeting Phillips is a mixture of customers and employees but also friends and neighbours, since he decided to buy a chalet in Snoqualmie Pass in

> "The physical draw of Evo's retail experience is clear – in Seattle, 40 per cent of orders are for in-store pick-up"

1

2

For those familiar with Evo, building homes as an extension of the brand shouldn't come as a surprise. Since 2013, Phillips has overseen expansion to urban markets in Denver and Portland, and opened satellite shops in mountain towns such as Hood River, Oregon. He has also acquired shops at Canadian resort Whistler and Japanese ski spots Furano, Haukba and Niseko. Another new Evo offering, Campus Salt Lake City, includes a hotel, skate park, climbing gym and restaurant. It's a model that Evo plans to replicate in Seattle and Tahoe City, California, as part of its vision to, as Phillips says, "create centres for the community to come together through customer-facing businesses". The result? In 2021, $201m (€199m) in revenue.

Evo's properties are often renovated industrial buildings – a 1910 mattress factory in Seattle, a 1927 auto building in Denver, an 1890s Salvation Army building in Portland and a 1935 inn at Lake Tahoe. Phillips sees their value as anchors for Evo's retail experience and knows that the outdoor adventure crowd is less one-dimensional than they appear. Yes, they are keen to hit the trail, but they can also appreciate a heritage building brought back to life with creative design. Evo's shops include spaces for exhibitions, film screenings, live music, talks and education classes on subjects such as avalanche safety. The physical draw is clear: in Seattle, 40 per cent of orders are for in-store pick-up.

"Whatever your line of business, you have to come from a place of being passionate about it," says Phillips. "We enjoy seeing and being a part of human connections. Customers can see whether the effort comes across as sincere or if it's just about bringing people together to sell more. They will always know if it's authentic." Given that Phillips is willing to live in one of his developments, we'd proffer that Evo's offering is. — GRS

2004. Used as a company retreat space, it prompted Phillips to purchase another home to live in with his family and was the genesis for The Pass Life. Here, under the direction of his property development arm Evolution Projects, he has built an environment for Evo enthusiasts to not only gather in shops and hospitality spaces but live too. The development includes a brewery and restaurant, an Evo satellite shop, a US Forest Service ranger station and 50 new homes – perfectly capturing Phillips' ambition to be where his customers are.

1.
Residential units at The Pass Life
2.
Prepping for a hike outside The Pass Life's restaurant

Toolkit takeaway
Selling online is cost effective but founding a town isn't. Despite this, Phillips established a neighbourhood for like-minded people (and fans of his brand) to meet, mingle and live.

In case of emergency…

When the going gets tough, a trusted ear is key to success

Even the canniest of entrepreneurs need someone they can call on for advice, insight and fresh thinking in an emergency. We asked five high-fliers and innovators to tell us who they turn to when things go south and share a little of the wisdom from their trusted confidantes. — CAG

Florian Idenburg,
Dutch architect and co-founder of SO–IL, USA
"I am fortunate enough to be able to turn to friends who operate in completely different professions, such as Charles van Es, who is chief sales officer at coconut water brand Vita Coco. He is removed from the day-to-day work of SO-IL and his advice allows me to look at things from a bigger perspective."

Lyn Harris
Co-founder of fragrance brand Perfumer H, UK
"I go to my family, including Christophe – my other half and CEO – because he's wise and we've been through lots together. His best tip? Stay focused on what you're good at."

Philippe Zuber
CEO of hotel group Kerzner International, UAE
"My sons Arsène and Archibald are part of a trusted group of people with whom I discuss ideas. They give me outsiders' opinions, which provide me with diverse perspectives."

Joyce Wang
Founder of interior designer Joyce Wang Studio, Hong Kong
"I often turn to my good friend, jewellery designer Nicholas Lieou for help on how to approach sensitive topics and situations, like when to stand up for myself and stand up for the studio."

Garrett Leight
Founder of eyewear brand Garrett Leight, USA
"My father [Larry Leight of Oliver Peoples] is one of the best at getting through to me. I can sum up the many things I've been taught as: crisis creates opportunity, prepare for the worst and hope for the best."

Q&A
Dax Dasilva
Canada

Dax Dasilva is founder of Montréal-based Lightspeed. The technology firm provides point-of-sale software for retailers and restaurants, helping them manage inventory, sell online and connect with suppliers and customers. Here, he tells MONOCLE how an art history graduate can start a CA\$2.5bn (€1.9bn) company. — NM

Lightspeed was a software developed to work with Apple's hardware. How did you spot a gap in the market?
When Apple started roaring back in the mid-2000s, I saw that people wanted to use its products in their businesses. Apple was humanising computers but what was lacking was powerful software to go along with its hardware solutions. I realised this was a ripe area to enter and meet the needs of people who wanted to use a Mac but couldn't.

Did this inspiration from Apple come across in the software?
The first versions were like iTunes for your shop or restaurant. So when people looked at the software, they immediately felt comfortable with it. And then of course, we added really slick design.

Why is design critical to tech products?
I quit computer science at university to study art history so Lightspeed didn't come from me being a great engineer; it was about design. I worked with an icon designer in Japan and we initially sold Lightspeed on its looks, before word of mouth meant that it started selling because of its power.

For more snappy business stories and interviews, tune in to Monocle 24's 'The Entrepreneurs' at monocle.com/radio.

Word on the street
Business books that should be written

As anyone whose eyes have ever glazed over while contemplating the shelves of an airport bookshop will know, the canon of business literature is vast. Some of it is probably even helpful, though it is always worth bearing in mind that the person who actually has figured out – as the title might suggest – how to make a billion euros without bestirring from their hammock is probably actually doing it, rather than cranking out large-print volumes explaining how *you* could (unless, of course, the production of such literature actually is their business model, in which case fair play to them).

But business books, like all self-help books, are peddling a fantasy: that if you will only do as this volume instructs, you will transcend your present misfortune and realise your dreams. All of which is easier said than done.

What is sorely lacking is a category of books that guide the budding tycoon through business as it actually is. All of the following, if anybody wants to go ahead and write them, would be valuable additions to the sum of wisdom on this subject. — AM

Fank You For Wuvving Our Pwoduct
Creating Customer Loyalty Through Infantilisation

A lexicon of the currently voguish corporate cutesiness which, while it drives all right-thinking citizens to paroxysms of rage, will make your enterprise incredibly popular with the kind of people who decorate their homes with uplifting affirmations rendered in florid typefaces.

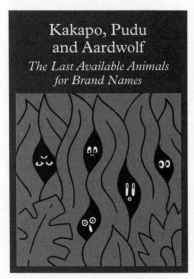

Kakapo, Pudu and Aardwolf
The Last Available Animals for Brand Names

Field guide to fauna so obscure that (at time of writing) nobody has as yet co-opted them into an insufferably twee brand name or trademark. Every entry annotated with rigorous profiling to ensure that the exotic creature in question is absolutely the right fit for your exciting new laundry app.

You Can't Take It With You, Grandad
Negotiating That Early Inheritance

A compendium of techniques for persuading elderly and/or infirm relatives to underwrite your professional (and personal) ambitions sooner rather than later. Schemes range from rigorously rational analyses of tax breaks to unadorned psychological warfare.

Delusion vs Inspiration
A Primer of Empowerment

Self-help guide for those stricken – very probably with good reason – by fear that if their idea was actually any good, or even remotely plausible, or at least not obviously idiotic, someone else would already have had it. Sample chapter: "They Probably Laughed at the Wheel".

ILLUSTRATOR: DIRK SCHMIDT

If These Jackasses Did It, So Can You
Obvious Clowns Who Made It Big

A cure for impostor syndrome in the form of heart-warming profiles of an assortment of outright dunces, flagrant chancers and just awful, awful people who nevertheless became enormously successful. You're better than these people, so you can surely be at least as rich.

Floggings Continue Until Morale Improves
Leadership Lessons From the Barbary Pirates

Treatise on management leaning into the buccaneering self-image often cultivated by the less bearable modern entrepreneur. A guide to transforming yourself into the equivalent of a scimitar-swishing corsair, terrorising your underlings just short of the point at which they make you walk the plank.

Yelp! I Need Somebody
The Theory and Practice of Rigging Online Reviews

A useful exploration of how to subtly swarm online review sites with delirious encomiums to your own product or service, and vicious disparagement of the offerings of your rivals. "Five stars, better than all other books on the same subject, which are written by morons" – *Goodreads*.

Bullshit Bingo
A Fun Game for Busy Entrepreneurs

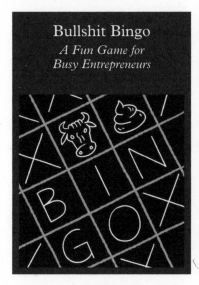

Not a book but a collection of bingo cards featuring words such as "synergy", "deliverables" and "stakeholder", which you can cross off as they come up in boring meetings. The prize, on emitting the exclamation associated with completing a row, is never being invited back.

Better Luck Next Time
Inspirational Tales of Recovered Bankrupts

Potted biographies of entrepreneurs who swung and missed at least once before finally striking it big. The usefulness of the advice is sadly offset by an overwhelming air of smugness as contributors dictate, between rueful chuckles, tales of their early failures from the deck of their yacht.

Hey, You've Earned It
Extradition Treaties and the Countries That Don't Have Them

A breezy guide to discreet and/or helpfully chaotic international locations which will welcome you and what remains of your start-up capital after the tragic file-destroying fire in your accounts department that will take place sometime in the small hours of next Wednesday.

IMAGES: BENYA HEGENBARTH, PICHAN SUJARITSATIT

Kitted out
A furniture rental service offering sustainability and style.

"Having been in the furniture industry for decades, you see a lot of waste in the life cycle of products," says Chanintr Sirisant (*pictured*) founder of Thai retailer Chanintr. In a bid to improve this and make fine furniture more accessible, Sirisant is launching a furniture-subscription company in Bangkok this autumn. Called Spruce, it will allow customers to rent items from Chanintr's stock, which includes Scandinavian brands Menu and Louis Poulsen and Portugal's De La Espada, on a monthly basis, with dining chairs for as little as €6 and sofas starting at €27.

Sirisant foresees a range of potential customers, from property developers looking to furnish rentals and show units, to savvy consumers who want a living room statement piece that will fit a tighter budget. The flexible rental structure also allows more adventurous customers to swap in new pieces monthly, allowing them to experiment and see what works in their space.

Each item is dropped off, assembled and then installed by Spruce's team. The model, Sirisant hopes, will help to counter the desire to turn to cheap, mass-produced furniture while also improving the quality of people's living spaces. "We want to make it as easy as possible for our customers to live in a nice, personalised space as quickly as possible," he says – a cause and business model we certainly admire. — NXE

Toolkit takeaway
Lowering the barrier to entry for high-quality and high-end products can improve quality of life across the board. And it can be a great business model as well. Doing good can help you make good too.

SHOP WITH MONOCLE

Discover our exclusive products and collaborations
with brands we admire at The Monocle Shop in London,
Zürich, Tokyo, Hong Kong, Toronto and Los Angeles.

Or browse online at *monocle.com/shop*.

VIEWS FROM THE TOP

From the freewheeling founder of a Taiwanese scooter company to the president of Japan's perkiest coffee chain, we've tapped some of the world's savviest leaders for their insights into doing business better.

Libby Wadle
CEO, J Crew Group

Launched in 1983, New York-based J Crew enjoyed decades as a go-to retailer for clothes that were classic, approachable and a little aspirational. Then, with the arrival of former Gap CEO Mickey Drexler and star designer Jenna Lyons in the 2000s, the outfit turned from a slightly preppy brand into a fashion phenomenon. Eventually, however, customers decided that J Crew had become too big for its chinos. Lyons stepped down in 2017 and Drexler left two years later, with the company more than €1.6bn in debt. It filed for bankruptcy in May 2020 as the first US lockdowns began to bite.

Libby Wadle was named J Crew's CEO that autumn at the pandemic's peak and immediately sought to address the company's malaise. The firm converted its debt to equity and received a €400m loan in a restructuring deal with creditors. Wadle has already helped to bring sales back to growth but she knows that there is plenty more to do. First, she recruited Brendon Babenzien, former creative director of Supreme, to oversee the company's menswear line. Now she's reviving J Crew's beloved catalogues, rethinking the retail environment and reinvesting in the product. — JIR

What have the past two years been like?
A process. We're not fast fashion and we took our time to find the right balance. We had lost some of our old inspiration and energy: people didn't feel inspired either to work or to shop here. But we've found a new sweet spot by being ourselves and trying to reignite the flame around the brand.

How do you bring back that excitement?
One of the things that J Crew really invented was this idea of being "in good company". It started with the menswear business a long time ago, when we were collaborating with Barbour, Timex and Alden shoes. We're returning to that strategy this autumn, through a collaboration with French shirting specialist Marie Marot. We also opened a men's concept shop in New York to highlight Brendon's new designs.

Why was Babenzien the right fit to head up J Crew's menswear?
He hates the term "streetwear" but his roots are with Supreme. For me, though, the magic phrase attached to Brendon isn't Supreme; it's J Crew. He grew up with the brand on Long Island. We didn't have design leadership for a while and he's a very relevant designer. He understands what a more mature customer wants but also gets the younger generation.

In which menswear categories do you see the biggest opportunities to make your mark?
We're thinking about elevated everyday clothing. Non-denim trousers have come back as we're moving into a more dressed-up era and our suiting business is incredibly important.

We're sitting around a table full of old J Crew catalogues. Will they continue to play a part in this new chapter?
We are in the process of reintroducing them. They remain so inspiring. I don't think that anything can replace the printed page.

How crucial are your physical shops?
We have fewer shops than we did in the past but they remain important. We're really thinking about how shops can be our best representation because at one point they became diluted versions of the brand. We are playing around and trying new design ideas, considering better lighting and how we can reposition our fitting-room areas to make the experience slightly more collaborative. The service aspect is a big opportunity.

Cutting costs is one way to save money but you've started investing in better-quality materials. Is that a risk?
We now use European mills for almost our entire men's suiting line. It's the reason why the suits are so good. We also relaunched our men's washed shirting line with a finer-quality fabric because we wanted to bring back the magic of those intricate details that were stripped away over the years. It used to be easy to dilute the quality without it being noticed right away but over time that waters down your brand.
jcrew.com

Lessons learnt:
Sacrificing quality is an easy way to save money in the short term but try it too often and customers will notice. Wadle's approach to restoring J Crew's fortunes involves tempting them back with better fabrics, designs and shops.

How to... thrive at scale

Lessons learnt:
Being a big player doesn't mean you have to be formulaic and predictable. Doutor's coffee is flame-roasted for the best flavour – even though there are quicker, easier ways – and every aspect of the café environment is carefully considered.

Masanori Hoshino
President, Doutor Coffee

PHOTOGRAPHER: FUMINARI YOSHITSUGU

Every day in Japan half a million people pass through the doors of a Doutor coffee shop. With more than 1,000 branches, Doutor is Japan's largest home-grown café chain. Though its coffee-roasting business was started in 1962, its first café opened in Harajuku in 1980. Today the company imports 10,000 tonnes of beans a year and owns one of the largest coffee plantations in Hawaii; last year it had a turnover of ¥59.8bn (€428m). And its name? It comes from Rua Doutor Paulo Ferraz da Costa Águiar, the São Paulo street on which the company's founder, Hiromichi Toriba, once lived.

The man in charge today is Masanori Hoshino, who joined the company in 1983. He is president of Doutor Coffee, publicly listed in 2000, and its multibillion-euro parent business, Doutor Nichires Holdings, which also runs other Japanese café chains such as Hoshino Coffee and Excelsior. Here, Hoshino speaks to MONOCLE over a brew in the company's Shibuya headquarters. — FW

What's your usual Doutor order?
A blend coffee and a German hot dog.

Tell us a little about the company's backstory.
A good cup of coffee is a given but we also wanted to offer a place to relax. We started Doutor in a time of huge economic growth, when everyone was working hard and exhausted. Japan already had a long history of coffee-drinking and *kissaten* cafés but table service was standard back then and coffee was more of a luxury.

We wanted to introduce the idea of the self-service café. We estimated that the average worker had ¥1,000 (€7) to spend every day and that had to include lunch and cigarettes. We calculated that ¥150 (€1) was the amount that people would spend on a cup of coffee. So we worked backwards from this to create an operation that would allow us to offer coffee at that price.

How do you keep customers coming back when there are so many options?
Beyond function and efficiency, there are emotional values that aren't so easy to quantify – small details that customers might not even consciously notice. Our saucers are designed to keep the spoon in place when you lift the cup. Our iced-coffee glasses are specially made so that when you swirl the straw, the ice tinkles against the glass like a *furin* [wind chime], which is a cooling, relaxing summer sound for Japanese people. Our background music is specially curated for us to suit the mood and time of day. It's not a single thing that customers could put their finger on but they sense that the overall ambience is cosy.

Doutor has an admirably simple menu. Is that a deliberate choice?
One of the core pillars of our business is selling beans: we sell a wide variety, from Blue Mountain to mocha and Kilimanjaro. But in terms of the café menu, Doutor doesn't offer hundreds of options. Blended coffee is the standard.

Is there still room for growth in Japan or is the market saturated?
In terms of domestic growth, physical shop expansion will be limited: there isn't enough space for us and all our competitors to open new shops. That's why I'm telling our staff to think outside the box. The old model was to have a shop on the high street but we have pioneered openings in hospitals, petrol stations and so on.

How are you innovating?
We are always looking at ways to improve how to roast our beans. That happens at our two roasting facilities in Hyogo in western Japan and Chiba, close to Tokyo. Regular coffee consumption at home has grown in Japan in the past few years, which is good news for the industry. We have developed our own drip bags; it's an easy way to brew our coffee.

You have a mix of directly managed and franchised shops. How do you maintain quality control?
First, our franchise partners understand that quality is essential for a successful business. Second, since our franchisees are not the ones standing in the shop – it's mostly part-timers and students – we maintain quality with supervisors who each look after 15 to 20 shops. We run an internal competition for service and operation to keep everyone motivated.

You already have a Doutor outlet in Malaysia. Is further overseas expansion on the horizon?
We're thinking about Asia and China but there could also be opportunities in Europe and the US. There are challenges too. We want to stay true to our philosophy but also localise. We need to find a balance between those two values. Right now we're looking at Vietnam.
doutor.co.jp

David Bowd and Kevin O'Shea
Co-founders, Salt Hotels

Salt Hotels is one of the fastest-growing boutique-hospitality brands in the US, with eight properties across the country. Its success demonstrates how to grow a brand at speed without compromising on the details. In 2014 founders David Bowd and Kevin O'Shea (*both pictured, Bowd on right*) opened Salt House Inn in Massachusetts, combining B&B-style homeliness with international standards of service. Both had backgrounds in big operations – Bowd, a Brit, used to run London's Chiltern Firehouse and Chateau Marmont in Los Angeles, while his partner, O'Shea, began his career at Starwood Hotels & Resorts – but had to roll up their sleeves and take on everyday chores to get Salt's first project off the ground. That, they say, is an essential part of the business's identity. Salt works with investors across the US to create its hotels, typically in historic properties requiring a little resuscitation. And it's adding to its portfolio: a members' club in LA will soon open its doors and a bolthole in Nantucket will launch next year. — CL

Salt has expanded rapidly. How do you keep a brand coherent at that pace of growth?
DAVID BOWD: You need to have a clear definition of what you're setting out to create, hire the right people and stay involved as it grows. You should work with someone who understands every nuance of what you've created and why. They should be your shadow, so when you move on to the next project, it's totally consistent.

KEVIN O'SHEA: We can go from a small, historic B&B in Cape Cod to something like The Aster in Hollywood. For me, it's a matter of aesthetics. I'm inspired by the buildings that we work with and they inform the design narrative. That's what connects the dots between all of our projects.

How did Salt House Inn get off the ground?
DB: Kevin cooked the breakfasts and I cleaned the rooms. It was a tremendous amount of hard work and we learnt as much from our failures as from our successes. I've never been to big hotel conferences and tried to sell Salt in that way. It has always been through recommendations and people who have stayed with us saying, "We're doing a hotel project and want you on board."

How has that early experience helped you?
KO: We have a better understanding of our teams and what they're doing because we've done it all

ourselves. For instance, when we're making design decisions, I know what it takes to clean a bedroom so I'm very mindful of that when I'm choosing fabrics or flooring materials. Yes, it's about achieving the look that we want but also ensuring that it won't look terrible in five years.

Where are the hospitality opportunities now?
DB: The boutique sector is still small here in the US. So many cities have subpar hotel experiences that don't reflect the local culture. We open in Minneapolis next year; it's such a cool city with an incredible culinary scene and it's one of the cities with the most Fortune 500 companies in the US. But it doesn't have a true lifestyle hotel to stay at.

KO: There are so many untapped markets, especially outside urban areas. I see a lot of opportunity in the Midwest.

Many new hotels are taking cues from Airbnb, where guests check in and out without ever dealing with a member of staff. Is that a good model?
DB: That's not hospitality to me and certainly not what we are. My heart is in wanting to look after people. That said, it's important that they have choices and we encourage the front desk to assess what a guest wants. However, we need to communicate to our guests that we know the best restaurants, bars and shops in the area. It's very hard to do that in a non-service, fully technological environment.

You are about to open The Aster, a members' club in Los Angeles. Why now?
DB: A lot has changed about how people work and socialise post-pandemic, so we felt that it was a good time for this. The old clubs were the country clubs where the level of service was fantastic. And then came members' clubs, which were very trendy but the service declined as the design improved. We wanted to create something that did both.

Is The Aster a brand that will expand?
KO: We've talked about it. What's interesting for us is really getting to know our members: who loves a negroni at 16.00, for instance, and ensuring that it's ready for them before they get there. It's a kind of service and hospitality that David and I have always been passionate about. There are a lot of interesting opportunities to deliver on that in a way that you can't do with a normal hotel guest.
salthotels.com

How to… build from scratch

Lessons learnt:
O'Shea and Bowd say that building a business as a couple is rewarding but can be tricky. You need to understand what skills each of you brings to the table and set boundaries: it's healthy to remind your partner to stay in their lane.

How to... test your mettle

Lessons learnt:
Be comfortable with taking on a certain amount of risk. Standing out in a packed field with a clear differentiator means leaving your comfort zone and encouraging others to do the same. Luke says that he is comfortable with "risking it all".

Horace Luke
CEO, Gogoro

If the origin story of Gogoro's CEO, Horace Luke, could be distilled into one event, it might be a childhood trip to a market in Hong Kong's Wan Chai district. There his mother told him a saying about the three types of people in the world: those who wait for opportunities, the smart ones who create opportunities and the people who let those opportunities fly by.

There's little doubt that Luke, who co-founded mobility company Gogoro in 2011, falls in the "smart ones" category. The Taipei-based company's electric scooters are easy on the eye but it's under the hood where Gogoro is setting itself apart from its competitors. While most electric scooters need to be plugged in to charge – a process that can take several hours – Gogoro's simply need to be taken to one of the company's 11,000 "Gostations" across Taiwan, where you can swap an empty battery for one with full power. "Swapping batteries is the game changer that enables urban residents to adopt electric mobility," says Luke, who is dressed in black and wears round-framed glasses.

In a sign that business is zipping along in the right direction, Gogoro has already licensed its

> ## "If you don't do things at the right time, on the right topic, it's really difficult. Timing is probably the most important thing in entrepreneurship"

battery system to its Taiwanese counterparts for use in their vehicles. The company's focus is on Asia for now – mainly China, India and the region's southeast – but it hopes to expand further afield. In April, Gogoro became a publicly traded company on the Nasdaq in the US. In the second quarter of 2022, it posted $90.7m (€90.8m) in revenue despite the challenges of the pandemic and a global economic downturn.

Gogoro occupies four floors of a shiny, new office building in central Taipei (it also maintains another office in nearby Taoyuan City). The company offers a simple idea but one that is complex in execution. To ensure that the Gostations work perfectly, Gogoro's team of engineers developed a software system that uses artificial intelligence and machine learning to "smart-charge" batteries, while taking into account Taiwan's sometimes unstable power grid and difficult weather conditions (including typhoon season). Luke, who was born in Hong Kong but was raised and studied in the US, says that his passion for doing something about sustainability made him pivot to electric vehicles after a career spent largely in consumer goods with companies such as Microsoft and HTC.

"We started Gogoro with 27 desks, thinking that it was going to be an intellectual-property-creation or technology company that would outsource everything," says Luke. But he quickly realised that the company would have to build everything itself if it wanted to realise its ambitions. So he drew on skills that he had honed over more than 20 years in product design. "I'm a creator but at the same time I believe that my number-one value is more as a cheerleader and team builder," he says. "I create a platform for other people to create and then go in and make things that they probably don't think that they could have made without this platform. That's my biggest value."

Gogoro's self-declared pompom shaker is clearly ambitious about where he wants to take the company. Part of that process involves mastering the data that it has accrued through the more than 325 million battery swaps that have taken place since Gogoro launched its first scooter in 2015. Luke says that he sees the company becoming the Google or Android of urban smart mobility, providing partners with the infrastructure to run an electric-scooter network, while also offering its own version of the vehicle. The concept is so novel that some industry analysts have described the 2,000-person company as a battery-maker that sells scooters as a proof of concept.

Like many entrepreneurs, Luke says that there's an element of luck to Gogoro's success. He cites the example of how Microsoft developed a pocket computer in the early 2000s. It failed, despite the company pouring millions of dollars into the project, only for Apple to succeed with the iPhone several years later. "The timing has to be right," he adds. "If you don't do things at the right time, on the right topic, no matter how much you push, it's really difficult. Timing is probably the most important thing in entrepreneurship."

Gogoro's timing, it seems, has been impeccable. Major changes in battery design over the past 10 years have helped to make electric vehicles cheaper and more efficient, while consumer behaviours have also shifted. Recent climate-related disasters and spiralling energy costs are likely to provide an extra incentive for people to gravitate towards Gogoro. For Luke, electric vehicles are a chance to make the planet a better place. "That's what drives me every day," he says. — EH
gogoro.com

PHOTOGRAPHER: SEAN MARC LEE

Jo Malone
Founder, Jo Loves

Perfumer Jo Malone was already at the top of her field when she founded fragrance and cosmetics company Jo Loves in 2011. She had sold her first brand, Jo Malone London, to Estée Lauder in 1999 in what she calls "the deal of a lifetime" and had stepped down from her role as its creative director in 2006. But it's this new chapter in her career, which began after a five-year non-compete agreement, that seems to be throwing up the most surprises. "I'm pushing myself back into the arena of adventure," she says, sitting in the candlelit studio of the Jo Loves shop in west London. It's a gloomy day but she is all smiles, having just received some good business news.

Her new adventure involves a temporary move to Dubai for what she calls a belated "gap year". There she plans to pursue the many expansion opportunities coming the way of Jo Loves. "We're now in China, South Korea and Australia, and are about to open in several new markets in the next year," says Malone, who is no stranger to launching and scaling globally.

Malone could easily have retired and "gone to sit on a beach" after her initial brand success but her entrepreneurial instincts led her to keep exploring her enhanced sense of smell and search for new ways of telling stories through fragrance. That's why Jo Loves products stand out: they are infused with stories from Malone's life and her travels around the world. Her journeys across Asia, for instance, have inspired a new series of pomelo-infused fragrances that became instant bestsellers. Even more popular are her Fragrance Paintbrushes, which hold the scent in gel form and encourage customers to get creative by applying it to their bodies.

Jo Loves came into its own when Malone opened its first flagship on London's Elizabeth Street, a stone's throw away from the flower shop where she had worked as a 15-year-old apprentice. The shop reflects her world: all-white interiors, piles of fragrances on shelves, a candle studio at the back and a big bar at the centre, where customers can try on fragrances (think wine tasting but for perfumes). "When I brought the concept to Shanghai we had six camera crews filming within an hour and thousands of people queueing to try it out," says Malone. "That's when I started to see the business turn – when I started travelling."

But it hasn't always been a smooth ride. "I was so eager to create again that I made a lot of mistakes when I launched Jo Loves," she says. "I had four fragrances and no strategy. I wanted to quit every single day for the first few years." But Malone had learned the power of perseverance early on in her life. The daughter of a beautician mother and an artist father, who liked to gamble, she grew up on a council estate. "When I mention 'estate', people assume that it was somewhere like Downton Abbey; it wasn't," says Malone, who left school aged 15. "It was like the projects."

Her survival instinct has remained intact ever since. After selling her first company, Malone was diagnosed with cancer and given nine months to live (she is now cancer-free). During this time, she temporarily lost her superpower: her sense of smell. "But I fought it and was desperate to create again," she says.

Malone is ambitious about where she wants to take Jo Loves, with impact and scale at the forefront of her planning, hence the focus on international expansion. Bricks-and-mortar shops remain key. "People want theatre and entertainment," she says.

"When I launched Jo Loves, I had four fragrances and no strategy. I wanted to quit every single day for the first few years"

"If you just whack a lot of product on a wall and expect it to sell, it won't. It's why we're focusing on freestanding shops. We have to create a home wherever we go."

When asked about her next steps, she gives no definitive answer, though she insists that she is open to anything. Does that include new categories beyond perfume? "Possibly," she says. A fragrance exhibition that could sit in Dubai's Museum of the Future, for example? "Why not?" When collaborations with the hospitality industry are mentioned she mysteriously promises to deliver a product that has "never been seen in the market before".

With a renewed appetite for adventure, Malone remains confident and is far from done. "If I wait for someone to knock on my door, the moment will pass," she says. She advises people with good business ideas not to be overly hesitant. It's why, prior to the permanent move to Dubai, Malone and her husband, Gary Willcox, who is the CEO of Jo Loves, decided to go skydiving above the city's Palm Jumeirah. "I haven't been the same person since – all those fears, I left them on the plane." While skydiving might not be for everyone, any budding entrepreneur could learn from Malone's willingness to jump, literally, into the unknown. — NT
joloves.com

PHOTOGRAPHER: LILY BERTRAND-WEBB

Lessons learnt:
When your business is growing, you'll have to decide to sell, get a partner or borrow money. For Malone, borrowing wasn't an option. "Be cautious about partners or selling and being part of something without the full responsibility," she says.

TRUNK

DOES BUSINESS COACHING WORK?

Executive coaching has evolved from Jordan Belfort-style barking and chest-thumping into meditative mindfulness, helping even the most harried of managers to handle their workload and teams. Useful professional tool or fluffy mumbo jumbo? We sit down with three coaches for an appraisal.

Coaches don't just help athletes perform: top CEOs and aspiring business folk are also seeking tips to get ahead too. According to a 2020 report for the International Coaching Federation, executive or career coaching is a €2.8bn industry – and an unregulated one at that, so buyer beware. Globally, the number of coaches had shot up to 71,000 by the end of the past decade. Is this a case of "those who can't do, teach"? Would a customer be better off seeking therapy? Is this just management consultancy with Californian packaging and snake oil thrown in? MONOCLE sent three writers to find out. — Ⓜ

Breathing in
High Performing Coach, *Global*

Joel Burgess says that there's a big difference between counselling and the business coaching he offers. Even so, there's something therapeutic about our session. Clearly someone who takes care of himself, the physically fit, yet softly-spoken coach tells me that he focuses on breathing for the first five minutes of every class – a seemingly eternal period of time that's enough to slow the mind of even the busiest CEO, entrepreneur or, in this case, a rushed magazine editor. "The first

thing people tend to say afterwards is, 'Wow, I feel amazing,'" says Burgess, a professional business coach who also trains other coaches as managing director of High Performing Coach. He's right.

British but Madeira-based, Burgess criss-crosses Europe to train businesspeople. Some of the techniques his "holistic approach" employs echo those of a psychotherapist: teaching clients mastery of their own minds and to contemplate their decision-making. While counselling is about "determining the present from the past and unpacking trauma", Burgess says that his coaching looks forward.

Whether trying to stay at the top, climb the ladder or become a business coach themselves, clients come to Burgess for help. When we discuss meditation, the coach recalls a session with a CEO who'd just raised €12m for his venture but wasn't interested in "mumbo-jumbo" mindfulness. "I persisted and now he loves meditation because it allows him to work skilfully with his mind. He's less reactive." Taking a beat allows professionals to better assess tough situations when the wrong move can cost millions, he adds. "It might be as simple as saying, 'Can I get back to you on that?'"

For Burgess, an entrepreneur who moved into coaching after founding London-based food firm Nutrifix, no two clients are the same. Some come to him for help with a task, while others are there for the long haul. His customers are mostly managers. Rather than micromanaging, "The best managers teach their teams how to think," says Burgess.

I relay how I struggled when I was promoted from a writer to an editor and became suddenly responsible for managing unruly journalists – an occasionally temperamental bunch. He assures me that I'm not alone. Burgess invites me to consider the coder's dilemma (many of his clients are in tech). "You get these chief technology officers who, because they're the best at coding, rise up the ranks quickly," he says. "Suddenly they're given

> **"When you begin this journey you learn to take responsibility for your actions. I've seen huge changes in myself and in my clients"**

a team to manage and they think, 'I don't want to do that, I want to code.' But if the CTO is able to empower these engineers to work effectively, the engineers, the company and the CTO win."

The key to empowering those employees? Listening. "The best salespeople talk the least," he says, adding that those who listen learn to not just ask the right questions but to do so at the opportune moment. Developing that empathy will be appreciated by others. Burgess schools his trainees in asking "powerful questions": the ones we avoid asking because the answer might yield a response we'd rather not deal with, as opposed to the ones at the top of a self-regarding Linkedin poll.

He tells me about one client, a CEO with hundreds of staff, who was always a few minutes late to sessions. "By the fourth time, I challenged him on it," he says. He told the executive that his tardiness undervalued the coaching and asked where else in his life and work he was behaving like this. "It forced him to get radically honest with himself," adds Burgess, and to inject his company philosophy with much-needed accountability.

I've learned that training for professional improvement is worthwhile, even if it touches the occasional nerve. Burgess says that his job is rewarding. "When you begin this journey you learn to take responsibility for your actions," he says. "I've seen huge changes in me and in my clients: better health, better business, more happiness." — NSG

Burgess charges €23,000 for twice-monthly meetings over six months, a weekend retreat in Madeira and support over Whatsapp and email between sessions.

Enhanced thinking
New York Life Coaching, *New York*

I didn't expect to be thumping my chest or doing war chants à la *Wolf of Wall Street* but a session with Annie Lin on the Upper West Side of Manhattan was far less intense than I anticipated. After all, New York is a city of strivers. You don't have to look far to find an ad for an executive coach, the witch doctors of the working world, who smile out from magazine centrefolds promising to double – maybe triple! – salaries with their advice or propel their students to the top of the corporate pyramid.

Lin, however, is a different operator. She holds sessions in her home, a calming apartment decorated with carvings and artefacts gathered on her travels around the world, drawing on the teachings of the Tao to lead her clientele of CEOs to their higher purpose. "I believe in the power of coaching," says Lin, who was born in Taiwan and migrated away from a career in finance to what she describes as a calling. "It's about seeing a vision of your future self and letting that pull you forward. The only way to get out of uncertainty is to have a defined vision of the future. That's why 'positive thinking' is insufficient; it has to be more personal than that."

Lin makes no bones about her style being a mix of business and life coaching. "A lot of my clients call themselves perfectionists but they're actually scared," she says. "'What if things go wrong?' 'What if others judge me?' Accept that fear, I say – allow that to be your reality." There's

> **"A lot of my clients call themselves perfectionists but they're actually scared. Accept that fear, I say"**

no question that our 75-minute session has a whiff of therapy. Yet unlike the drier executive coaching of finding one's own "personal KPIs", she, like any good therapist, allows you to talk yourself into an "ah-ha" moment. In fact, once we started I wouldn't shut up.

Prior to meeting, Lin had sent a series of prompts for me. How satisfied was I with my career, wealth, education, relationships? What would a "10" look like for each? I wrote that I've always believed in letting my work speak for itself yet had the nagging feeling that that's diminishing in a world where everyone is fighting to be

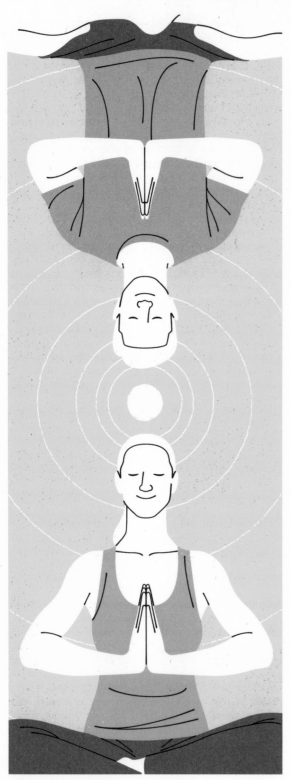

heard. Harping on in the Twittersphere has never been my thing, I explain in Lin's living room. I loathe writing bios; my website is pointedly plain. You want as many people as possible to read your writing but I've harboured a hang-up about online self-promotion – perhaps in part because MONOCLE has also been careful on this front.

I'd half expected Lin to say, "That's the way it is, sunshine; get with the programme," and come up with various encouragements and social media strategies. Instead, we talked through examples of those who I felt had successfully put themselves out there, online or offline. "Let's call it 'personal branding', rather than 'self-promotion'," she says, with a smile. "It just sounds less aggressive."

As we talk, we come to the notion of acting "in service of the work", which treads a fine line between self-help and corporatese, yet makes utter sense. We discuss a series of actionable things that I can do to make myself more visible online

"I believe in the power of coaching. It's about seeing a vision of your future self and letting that pull you forward"

without having to wade into the maelstrom of Twitter. "So which are you going to do in the next two weeks?" asks Lin. "Having specific actionable items, which I'll check in on after our session, is the main difference between this and therapy."

The second half of our session spills into the stresses of anticipating a big project and the nature of fear – chewy stuff. The way Lin coaches is not for everyone. If you're looking for someone who will dish out direct pointers on leadership strategies or nailing pitches, this isn't it. But she extols a humanistic attitude to work, seeing career as something that's shaped around your inner life, even the awkward bits; many people, I suspect, would benefit from that kind of thinking. More leaders in the workplace are being encouraged to show their vulnerability but it can get out of control: I think of one recent example of a CEO posting a tearful selfie on Linkedin about how hard it was to fire a bunch of people.

Nevertheless, everyone needs someone to talk to and, unlike a traditional therapist, Lin is someone who has boxed in the corporate ring too. Executive coaching, done right, can work. — CL

A three-month Annie Lin course is $2,200 (€2,200), meeting every two weeks.

Generational wisdom
Coaching Management Institute, *Seoul*

Letting your guard down with a stranger is rarely easy but on my call with former KB Insurance CEO Kim Byung-heon, who is now an executive coach, I find myself fidgeting in my chair more than usual. When you're asked to delve into your professional weaknesses by one of the country's former titans of finance, it's tempting to feel that your problems are small.

After some initial awkwardness, though, I find myself opening up. Following our session I realise that Kim has been encouraging me in subtle ways. Beaming through my screen from his personal library, he hasn't contradicted me once and has instead backed up my own assessments of my career. I'm not new to therapy but having a veteran businessperson empathise with me is validating, if not a little unsettling.

The history of executive coaching in South Korea is shorter than in the West but, coaches say, more leaders are recognising the need for their services as their companies go global. "Many firms have transformed from fast followers to first movers. This means that the companies that previously couldn't tolerate failures now must embrace and foster a culture that encourages them," says Kim, who spent more than 30 years in finance as well as in the strategy division at multinational conglomerate LG Corp. "Without a culture that allows taking risks, it's hard to attract world-class talent."

In that vein, there's plenty of demand for executive coaching in Asia's fourth-largest economy. South Korea is known for perfecting smartphones and container ships but foreign investors have long viewed its companies as lagging in corporate governance and culture. At the top of the country's largest conglomerates, professional managers revere the founders' descendants and often rely on the families' influence to push decisions through the boardroom, even though their stakes have been diluted significantly over decades of growth. Lower down the ladder, seniority can count as much as, if not more than, performance when it comes to promotions, and that frustrates millennials and Gen Z employees.

Seoul's Coaching Management Institute allows clients to benefit from the wisdom of former executives (90 per cent of its coaches have such experience). Helen Hyonsook Ko, the institute's founder and a management-studies professor at Seoul's Kookmin University, explains how the service differs from management consulting, comparing it to a discreet sounding board. "Consultants prescribe

solutions, whereas coaches prod you into thinking on your own," she says. Kim, who became a partner-coach after retiring from KB Insurance in 2015, adds that "in most cases, you already have the answer in your head".

In our session, Kim tells me that he advocates going back to basics and letting the client take the initiative. He asks me to talk about my personal priorities as well as the reasons behind a professional dilemma I've faced. He shares ordeals from his career that might resonate but stops short of making a direct comparison. Coaching, Kim says, gives clients the push "to make the difficult

> **"Consultants prescribe solutions, whereas coaches prod you into thinking on your own"**

changes that leaders lose sleep over" and it "gets you to stop and look at yourself critically". I certainly found that injection of perspective helpful.

There's something in it for the coaches too, besides their fee. "There was a retired CEO who used to joke that he was playing golf 100 days a year," says Kim, laughing. "Some of his peers decided to become coaches because they still have the drive to contribute and improve." — JSK

A session at Seoul's Coaching Management Institute costs between €700 and €1,000 per hour and the number of sessions depends on each client's needs.

1

2

LIFE IN THE SLOW LANE

Bored of big cities and tedious commutes? Considering jacking in your job and starting something new in a place with a gentler pace of life? We have just the idea: start up somewhere slower. We visit Mexico, Indonesia and Sicily to find out how it's done.

Open city
Guadalajara

Americana is one of Guadalajara's liveliest and most diverse neighbourhoods, where the gridded streets are lined with tall trees and old townhouses taken up with buzzy little bars and hotels. We're in the second most populous city in Mexico but you can still hear the birds chirp over the traffic and people move at an unhurried pace. Even the street-food vendors prepare workers' lunchtime *torta ahogadas* (sandwiches drowned in salsa) and fresh mango in a less flustered fashion than in Mexico City.

It's this big city's small-town feel and access to more affordable rent that has made the state capital of Jalisco a hotspot for entrepreneurs from Mexico, the US and further afield, all seeking a better quality of life. Between 2010 and 2020, the population in Guadalajara ballooned by 18 per cent to about 5.2 million. Since the pandemic began, the pace of arrivals has soared, partly because the cost of living in the capital, 550km to the southeast, has risen vertiginously.

1.
Piedrafeugo
2.
Guadalajara
90210
3.
Designer
Fabien
Cappello
4.
Artist Jorge
Méndez Blake
5.
Capello's
studio
6.
Edurne
and Mirren
Navarro
of Karmele

Part of the city's allure is its bohemian artistic past as the birthplace of creative giants including architect Luis Barragán – a legacy that has endured to this day. "Here it is a community," says artist Jorge Méndez Blake about the city's buzzing creative scene. "We all go to the same framer." Méndez Blake was born and raised here but is part of a large and growing number of self-employed artists availing themselves of affordable studio space.

José Noé Suro, the founder of the Cerámica Suro factory, has worked with everyone from Ghanaian-British architect David Adjaye to artist Jorge Pardo and painter Sarah Crowner. He has been instrumental in drawing attention to the city, which he likens to Los Angeles in part because of the surrounding sierra.

"The scene here has a strong identity and that goes back to Barragán," says Aldo Alvarez Tostado, founder of homeware brand Piedrafeugo. At the new showroom, there's also a residency space and a courtyard where Tostado hosts art events. It's one of the many new spaces to have opened recently.

PHOTOGRAPHERS: ANA HOP

4

3

5

6

"It's very
attractive
to live in a
connected
city with
a big
cultural
scene"

While the traffic isn't bad, getting around is also easier now that the city has a third metro line, which was added in 2020. Its construction cost more than €1.5bn, making the line the largest investment project in the history of Jalisco state. Meanwhile, the airport now serves more than 25 international destinations with direct flights from cities including Los Angeles, Panama City and Madrid, with a Colombia connection set to be added this year. The once-traditional city has become much more outward looking in part thanks to vastly improved internet access, a less conservative government since 2009 and an influx of new people.

"I can feel the change," says Alberto Lopez Corcuera, an artist who recently opened Guadalajara 90210, a contemporary art space in a former school in Colonia Americana. "Guadalajara used to be a

1

2

super traditional city but in the past five or so years, everything has changed. The new generation is much more open."

French designer Fabien Cappello, who relocated from London by way of Mexico City, agrees. "It's very attractive to live in a connected city with a big cultural scene," he says. Cappello followed his partner to Guadalajara and now works in a spacious, colourful, plant-filled studio in Alcalde Barranquitas, a quiet working-class neighbourhood just north of the city centre. "The older generation put Guadalajara on the map and now the younger generation can imagine creating within the city. That's what convinced me that I could move here."

The hospitality scene has improved too, with the opening of Grupo Habita's comely Casa Habita hotel in Americana. "It doesn't feel so saturated," says Diego Villaneuva Plascencia, owner of Zuno Café, set in a mansion house in Americana. He moved here from Mexico City, where he had a popular design shop called Apt 25 in La Roma. He's sitting in the banana-palm-filled courtyard of Zuno, on a yellow wire chair designed by his friend Cappello. "A lot of visitors are coming here and they don't want to feel like they're in Brooklyn," he says, referencing the increasing Americanisation of the capital. At the front of the house, in a space that spills onto a tiled terrace, he recently opened the second Apt 25 shop, a beautiful wood-panelled room with royal blue carpets and shelves with goods such as ceramics by local creatives, as well as a few international brands. He hopes to acquire the rest of the mansion and open another restaurant in the coming months.

While many outsiders have rolled in, the restaurant is largely run by *tapatíos*

3

4 5

6

7

(Jalisco natives), who never left or decided to move back home after honing their trade abroad, says José Alonso Martin Ocampo, partner of restaurant group Grupo Habana Negrita.

"We now have people coming here with cool ideas looking for places like this," he says, gesturing to Salon Candela, an open-air cantina in the Seattle neighbourhood. A few streets away is Enora, a new coffee shop and restaurant that spills out onto a wide pedestrian-centred avenue opened by partners from the Risoma network. The locally founded group has a collection of cult restaurants including De La O and Pal Real.

Karmele, a bakery with exposed cement walls, wood shelves and basket lights, was opened by sisters Edurne and Mirren Navarro. Mirren, who recently did a stint at Hart Bageri in Copenhagen, launched her own bakery in her parents' house in 2019. Today there's a queue for freshly baked goods such as baguettes, cheesecake, cookies and *Karmelitos* (a riff on the Breton *kouign-amman* pastry), oozing with berries and chocolate.

But for all its new places and people, Guadalajara maintains a distinct identity. At Xokol, a restaurant in Santa Teresita run by two of the city's youngest rising chefs, Óscar Segundo and Xrysw Ruelas, there's something that feels close to the essence of what's good about Guadalajara. The neighbourhood is full of tradition but close enough to affluent areas to be successful, says Ruelas. The restaurant, which recently moved, now has slick charcoal-coloured walls, a long, shared dining table and a vast open kitchen, where diners catch whiffs of smoke from the wood oven and open *comal* (clay griddle). It's by far the most polished spot to open in the area but that seems to suit people: as does the nod to pre-colonial culinary customs and the use of heirloom corn from Segundo's grandmother, whose portrait is proudly daubed on the wall.

"Whenever I'm at Óscar's mom's house, she gives me a tortilla as a welcome," says Ruelas. Around the dining table it's mostly families; way after 22.00, there's a queue out of the door. "More and more people are moving to Guadalajara," says Ruelas. "It's a city that has so many opportunities." — MHO

1

Sunshine state
Bali

Until 2020, the Argentinian architect Dolores Giribone had never been to Asia. Then she met Peter Witkamp, a Dutch entrepreneur who was passing through Buenos Aires. "We started dating and right away he said he wanted to move to Indonesia," says Giribone, who is sitting in the shade of her palm-fringed villa in northern Bali.

Witkamp, who was setting up a socially conscious investment firm, convinced her how easy it could be to work from there. After stopovers in the Netherlands and North Macedonia, they moved to Ubud, a tranquil town in the hills of the tropical island in 2021. Giribone hasn't looked back since.

1.
Puri
Saraswati
Dijiwa
in Ubud
2.
The path to
fulfilment?
3.
Shrey
Gaurishankar
in Apsara
4.
Dinner
at Apsara
5.
Alchemy
restaurant
in Ubud
6.
Canggu
natural wine
bar Mosto

Tourism to Bali cratered during the initial shock of the pandemic but now that borders are open again, the easy-going, mainly Hindu island, long beloved by surfers and hippies, is experiencing a new wave of remote workers and entrepreneurs. Some are seeking sunshine and a higher quality of life as they pursue careers; others are founding start-ups and raising families with the intention of staying. "What makes Bali special is that it's like a meeting incubator," says Giribone. "Everyone has your back and is there to help you."

Shortly after arriving, Giribone joined architecture firm Pablo Luna Studio and then co-founded a Bali-based jewellery line. Meanwhile, Witkamp co-founded Katalys, which helps start-ups, but is also the programme director of the Borneo Initiative, a rainforest

conservation group. They work from home in a villa, which has a pool, and take business meetings at beach clubs around the island. Giribone's studio, which is surrounded by trees and terraced rice fields. On the weekends they head to the beaches in the south or venture north for the mountains and waterfalls.

"Bali definitely gives people the opportunity to reset professionally, and you can really start something completely new if you'd like to as well," says Shrey Gaurishankar, who relocated to Ubud in 2021 after working in executive search and recruitment in Singapore. He opened Indian restaurant Apsara last December and this September he launched a second venture down the street: by day, it's Tucky, a speciality coffee shop, while at night it transforms into Bacari, a sleek wine bar.

"The quality of life as opposed to a city like Singapore is very different," says Gaurishankar. "Because of the more laid-back pace, you feel a lot more present, you feel a lot more relaxed. You're a lot more surrounded by nature. And you end up meeting a lot of creative people from different walks of life."

Before the pandemic, co-working spaces were a natural meeting place for people who needed only their laptops to work and fields such as graphic design and digital marketing tended to be

1

over-represented. Since Indonesia's borders fully reopened earlier this year, co-
working companies in Bali have welcomed
a more diverse range of remote workers
back to their sunny office spaces.

David Abraham, co-founder of
Outpost, a coworking and co-living company, says that its Ubud and Canggu
branches are back to more than 90 per cent
capacity and he's noticed that there are
more families and more first-time travellers
coming in. Outpost's locations are open 24
hours a day to accommodate the employees
of firms operating in European or North
American time zones. "People don't want
to put off their bucket list destinations
any more," says Abraham.

Eddie Jaoude and Sara Abou-Jaoude
are two such newcomers. Sara, a former
lawyer, left her job to join her husband
in his web-development business. The
couple left the UK for Canggu in late
2021 after months of searching to find
somewhere inexpensive, attractive and
exciting. "We researched Bali a lot and
we realised that it has obviously great
weather and great food but also a big
digital community – so good internet
speeds and a lot of entrepreneurial people,"
says Sara. "We thought it seemed like an
amazing destination."

She now spends her weekends
discovering the further-flung corners of
the island, exploring the area by scooter.

2

Moving to Bali:
The basics

Length of time it takes to register a business here:
Four to six weeks. Some companies, like Emerhub, promise just four weeks.

Commercial rent per sq m:
€175 per month for an unlimited pass at Outpost Co-working. About €1,000 for a 55 sq m commercial property in Canggu.

Number of new arrivals:
There were approaching 250,000 international arrivals in May 2022 alone.

Key growth industries:
Eco-tourism, technology, fashion, wellness, health tourism.

Average cost of renting:
In Ubud, a two-bedroom villa is IDR15m (€1,000) a month.

Average length of commute:
Traffic can be bad across the island so most people who work in an office are in the same town.

Hours of sunshine a year:
3,137 a year in Canggu; slightly fewer in Ubud.

One advantage to living here:
Community of expatriates and entrepreneurs; access to nature.

One disadvantage:
Flights from Denpasar offer good connectivity in Asia but less so for longer-haul journeys.

1.
Kimiko Aida at Missibu Roaster and Showroom
2.
Pool at Outpost Co-working in Ubud
3.
Tending bar at Mosto

4.
Model business
5.
Dolores Giribone and Peter Witkamp in Ubud

3

4

5

"For both of us, food and weather are major points," says Sara. "I obviously knew we needed to go to a place where we could get our work done, but also have a good quality of life. Bali really stood out. Sometimes when you travel you might feel a little bit displaced or you always feel like a tourist in a particular area – but you don't in Bali; that's a real advantage of the island."

It's not just foreigners who are realising Bali's potential. "Now we have more local entrepreneurs in the coworking space, a lot of people from Jakarta," says Hasina Mahary, a consultant for Dojo Bali Coworking in Canggu. "I think it was a realisation of the better balance that Bali can offer."

There is a whole industry in Bali dedicated to helping foreigners obtain visas

> ### "We needed to go to a place where we could get our work done but also have a good quality of life"

to work in Indonesia, where agents help arrivals sort the sometimes arduous paperwork and ensure that they meet the legal requirements. In June, Indonesia's tourism minister Sandiaga Uno said that the country is preparing a five-year visa for remote workers, with no tax obligations payable on foreign-earned income. The government is expected to launch the scheme this year – and there is plenty of interest that it actually does.

Although many people arrive with intentions of staying a short while, others end up putting down deeper roots than they first intended. In 2019, when her eldest son turned six, Kimiko Aida left Tokyo for Canggu. She enrolled her children in school and appreciated the environmentally-focused approach to learning over the stricter conventional education that her children would be getting back in Japan. For work, she remotely manages a coffee farm in Kagoshima and she now plans to start a coffee consultancy from Bali. "I don't want to go back to Japan," she says, with a smile. "Tokyo is too crowded." — NXE

1

2

Southern comforts
Catania

"We used to see Sicily as an example of how business should not be done, or we just associate it with folklore," says Catania-born Enrica Arena, CEO of Orange Fiber, a company that turns the by-product of citrus juice into sustainable textiles. "Now we're trying to change that narrative."

Catania, perched at the foot of Europe's most active volcano, is Sicily's second city. Like much of southern Italy it has long been a desirable, languid and lovely place to live but perhaps less somewhere to run an efficient business. Like Mount Etna itself, though, there's a pressure bubbling beneath the surface and that change is beginning to burst forth as a crop of new fashion and manufacturing businesses.

1.
Cathedral of
Sant'Agata
2.
The Le
Pannier team
3.
Church
in Acireale
4.
Out and about
5.
Workshop
used by
Pierfrancesco
Virlinzi
6.
Nanna Pause

Enrica Arena studied in Milan and worked with the UN in Egypt before she decided to return home and co-found her start-up in 2014. As about 61 per cent of Italy's oranges are grown in Sicily, a proximity to the island's groves was useful for her citrus-focused firm. Having collaborated with retail giants such as H&M, Orange Fiber boasts the sort of brand recognition that draws in people from the rest of Italy too. "Many of our employees come to us," says Arena of the once-daunting task of tempting talent here from the mainland.

In an atelier-cum-gallery only a few metres away from the co-working space where Orange Fiber is based, Marella Ferrera is applying the finishing touches to a custom-made wedding dress. The Catania-born designer worked in Rome making opera costumes for clients in Greece and Spain, then in Milan before moving home to start her atelier. Her dresses, some of which are made using scraps of volcanic rock and ceramics from nearby town Caltagirone, are inspired by Sicilian culture and craft. "The island has real soul," she says, looping a final stitch into an errant hem.

Ferrera and Arena are discussing a partnership, combining the former's design know-how with Orange Fiber's textiles. A good illustration of how the age-old craft of making a wedding dress might benefit from the fresh businesses moving in.

3

4

5   6

Moving to Catania: The basics

Length of time it takes to register a business here:
About 5 to 7 days.

Commercial rent per sq m:
About €12 a month.

Key growth industries:
Fashion, textiles and manufacturing.

Average cost of renting a home:
A one-bedroom city-centre apartment costs about €570 a month.

Hours of sunshine:
2,433 a year.

One advantage to living here:
There's a close-knit community of creatives.

One disadvantage:
Not a lot of support for businesses from the municipal government.

1 2

3

4

5

"The brand is about our past, heritage and traditions. We had to stay here"

Also making waves is Pierfrancesco Virlinzi's swimwear brand Pier Sicilia, which started in 2019. "In the past it was common to have all your suits, shirts, underwear and, of course, bathing suits tailored," says a beaming Virlinzi, in his workshop. Through his label, Catania-born Virlinzi hopes to bring the same high standard back into swimwear design. The fact that he has ample opportunities for a swim in the Mediterranean during his lunch breaks is also a perk.

In Acireale, a city north of Catania, the scale of opportunity on the island appears bigger than small businesses and one-person ateliers. Le Panier makes about 1,500 leather accessories a month, combining age-old know-how with new technology to create prototypes and leather goods for major luxury brands. Not long ago, many businesses like this appeared doomed to lose out to cheaper labour abroad. But one silver lining to the current economic stalemate with China and logistical snarl-ups is that many brands are reshoring their manufacturing. Le Panier's idyllic location? That's a bonus for visiting designers and the staff here. "The ocean is just around the corner," says co-founder Rosario Michele – who, ever the entrepreneur, also owns a nearby gelato parlour. "I often go for a lunchtime swim."

As well as a shift towards making things at home, more transparent supply chains and an onus on better working conditions,

1.
Salvatore and Elena Laura Zingales
2.
Mount Etna
3.
Inspecting Orange Fiber's textiles
4.
Restaurants opposite the fish market
5.
A relaxed Virlinzi
6.
Marella Ferrera puts the finishing touches to a Sicilian veil

money from the EU's €800bn post-pandemic Next Generation fund is now up for grabs for sustainably-minded companies with a green focus.

North of Catania in Mirto, nestled between olive groves and thickets of prickly pears, Salvatore Zingales' workshop specialises in the production of double-face coats. Sown using a weaving technique that creates two layers on the same fabric, the complex method makes for warmer, higher-quality jackets. While this kind of craftsmanship has become associated with workshops in Italy's north, Zingales and his team are intent on proving that the South's tailoring traditions are just as strong – and that companies here can be just as productive. The business employs more than 200 seamstresses in the area, all of whom produce items for luxury brands including Max Mara and Bottega Veneta, plus smaller firms including the Paris-based Nanna Pause.

Over the years, designer Nanna Pause has established a close connection with Zingales and the workshop's seamstresses. "When something goes wrong, being able to call and talk to the person making that particular item is very helpful," says Pause as the sun begins to set on the dusty track that leads to the workshop.

This generation of Catania creatives continues to bring back production and start homegrown labels. "When I started my brand, people asked me why I didn't want to just produce abroad in Turkey or Portugal," says Virlinzi, in sight of the mighty volcano which presides over Catania. "But the brand is about our past, heritage and traditions. We had to stay here." Listen closely: perhaps you'll hear the rumble of change too. — CAG

6

KONFEKT

1

DINING

Flavours of the season

2

FASHION

Essential outfits for autumn

These potato galettes with sheep's yoghurt are one of many delicious ideas served up in the magazine.

ISSUE 8 —— AUTUMN

It's the season for chunky knits, sturdy shoes and rich reds, browns and greens. Whatever the time of year, *Konfekt* offers inspiration for how to fill your wardrobe with style and sophistication.

3

REGIMES

Be well,
stay well

4

TRAVEL

Perspectives
on the world

5

DESIGN

Objects
of desire

Konfekt takes tips from those who know how to escape, such as artist Anna Kuen, who rides to a lake outside Berlin to swim and refuel.

Peek inside the world's most beautiful and unusual residences and meet the interiors geniuses that created them in *Konfekt*'s aspirational design section.

Konfekt's writers and photographers criss-cross the globe finding the best stays – and making friends.

Inspiring itineraries, debates & recipes

SUBSCRIBE NOW —— KONFEKTMAGAZINE.COM

GOOD BUSINESS, ONLY BETTER

Just as the global economy is in a state of flux, our ideas about what makes a successful entrepreneur are ripe for re-evaluation. We hear from seven savvy voices about universal constants in commerce and the key elements for success in the new world of enterprise. **ILLUSTRATOR** *Giordano Poloni*

Death of the charismatic founder
by Michel Hogan

A string of recent high-profile falls from grace has underscored the importance of humility in business. It also shows how the notion of the visionary founder is, well, foundering.

During recent years, a generation of huckster entrepreneurs has finally got its comeuppance, and observing its members' falls from grace can teach us all a lesson. The downfall of Wework's Adam Neumann and Uber's Travis Kalanick, as well as the conviction of Elizabeth Holmes, whose Theranos health start-up falsified blood tests, suggest a timely swing against the fêted founders inflated by messianic zeal.

I work on making brands stick and I don't think that a cult of personality can ever be a proxy for good leadership. To me, the idea of the visionary entrepreneur singlehandedly changing the world is both irksome and clichéd, and ignores the mountain of other people's (often unheroic) work that usually underpins such success. Unfortunately, blind hubris and unchecked excess are hardly new and they don't just affect start-ups. Luckily, however, now feels like a good moment to challenge it and consider what can take the place of this unhelpful trope.

Founders with Hindenburg-sized egos float at first but they often end up blowing up their beloved endeavours entirely. In doing so, they have ignored a few of the most tried and trusted building blocks of management: avoiding the hot air of hype, the pursuit of sustainable growth and taking a rational view of risk and fallibility. Whether you're running a shop in a one-horse town or riding in on a unicorn, entrepreneurs ignore these simple principles at their peril.

In the past few years there has also been something of a positive move to hold more and more of these charismatic but badly behaved founders to account, which can only be a good thing. Now, more than ever, if you misbehave your board is likely to show you the door. This feels like a much better balance than in bygone years.

Still, it is too simplistic to lump all entrepreneurs together. The notorious few might inspire headlines and television shows but there remains a quiet majority of businesses that continue to steadily bank value with honest intent. As for mainstream role models who sum up the simple, sober antidotes to the excesses of founder culture? Well, the man behind clothing company Patagonia, Yvon Chouinard, is an example of someone who has managed to build a sustainable company with a stellar reputation.

Such entrepreneurs understand that brands accumulate value by making promises they can keep and not by relying on grandiose ideas and pure self-confidence to justify iffy short-cuts or missteps. Good leaders still need a clear sense of who they are but must also combine it with a purpose and set of values that they make widely understood to their staff. It's this that shapes the day-to-day workings of a company.

We should also remember that what propels a business – at any size and stage – is the everyday work that balances the books, cares for customers and colleagues, and sorts the product. Then does it all over again the next day. The grandstanding and glamorous bits of any job rarely make up the majority of people's work.

Perhaps it is time to consider a different crop of entrepreneurs: the sort of people who have the confidence to ditch dreams of world domination, zillion-dollar valuations and ego-inflating articles in favour of more modest and meaningful goals. The sort whose success isn't defined by making the magazine covers or having a television show made about them.

If you ask me, it is time to bury the idea of the iconic, faultless and charismatic founder, the person who built an empire on an idea, amassed impossible wealth and power, and avoided the failures that colonise the path to success. We should also ask ourselves, honestly, if these mythical beings have ever really existed or whether we have created them ourselves.

By sharing those stories, we can perhaps elevate a different type of founder: entrepreneurs with the confidence to forego shallow, self-aggrandising fantasies and instead lead sustainable businesses that contribute to a better world. — Ⓜ

About the writer: Hogan is an Australia-based business adviser who helps companies large and small to avoid the risk of making the wrong promises. She is also a regular contributor to various publications and the author of the book *The Unheroic Work*.

Out of the frying pan...
by Charmain Ponnuthurai

A successful venture begins with an idea that inspires you, coupled with the impulse to pursue it. But you also need focus, the humility to learn from your mistakes – and plenty of tenacity.

Entrepreneurship is like writing a poem: it's about following a feeling. My immersion in the world of food began 20 years ago when I worked part-time co-ordinating events at a shop called Books for Cooks in west London. It was a place to discuss ingredients, tastes and food. Inspired by that time, I compiled *Midnight Feasts: An Anthology of Late-Night Munchies* and donated the proceeds to a dyslexia charity called Springboard.

I tried to involve French cookware giant Le Creuset, which had brought out a range of items in midnight blue. The company never responded but the experience inspired my own business, Crane, and its first prototype for a milk pan. We crowdfunded its creation and selected an old foundry in France to start production. What I'll say to people who want to start something similar is

It was all very serendipitous and organic, despite our lack of a proper marketing budget

that the cookware market is hard to crack and is full of established players. I remember talking to staff at our induction day – no pun intended – at Harrods about why they should sell our four pans in a room crowded with pieces by Staub and Le Creuset.

We sent pans to cooks and chefs around London and Crane's sales grew by word of mouth. MONOCLE even gave us our first press feature. It was all very serendipitous and organic, despite our lack of a proper marketing budget. At the time we didn't even have packaging materials, such as printed boxes in which to send out the pans – just stickers.

In the eight years since, I have learned a lot and, like all entrepreneurs, made some mistakes. We were behind the curve of direct-to-consumer cookware brands coming up in the US; at the time we were wholesaling to shops and were too slow to adapt. This year we encountered supply-chain issues with our stainless-steel pans. We have had to deal with factories closing and long delays. I'm

What makes an entrepreneur?
by Stefan Allesch-Taylor

There are a million and one guides supposedly offering the keys to success, so sometimes it's good to revisit the simple, core elements of building a business.

I have often been asked what makes a good entrepreneur. For many "experts" the answer always includes the same never-give-up clichés. But there's much more to think about today than steely determination. There's an economic tempest raging: supply chain problems, workforce shortages, high inflation, a climate crisis and war.

These are far from the challenges that others faced, even five years ago. I've found that the forces that make a successful entrepreneur vary with the times. For those looking to start up right now, though, here is my advice:

1. **Give people what they want.**
Research from CB Insights shows that 42 per cent of businesses that fail do so because no one wanted their product or service in the first place. Listen to your biggest critics: they are your most valuable asset. If you can answer the naysayers, you're off to a good start.

2. **Hire well.**
Lousy hires destroy the very best ideas. I would advise any entrepreneur to get a good understanding of human resources – not just to ensure the swift exit of a "bad fit" but also to understand more about team building and motivation strategies beyond just money.

3. **Make friends.**
No entrepreneur is an island. Don't embark on any venture if you haven't built up a network of people who are already engaged in your market or have the skills that your business needs to get moving. You're not proselytising; you're motivating the people who share your vision and believe in your start-up.

4. **Prioritise messaging.**
Too often I see 90 per cent of budgets go on development and very little on marketing. Business titan Andrew Carnegie wrote, "If I had $10,000 to start a business, I'd spend $1,000 on the product and $9,000 on marketing." And it is not just algorithmic ads; it needs a bit of "you" and a bit of magic dust to stand out from the dross. The overwhelming majority of internet traffic goes to a handful of websites. Think about how you're going to be heard and seen.

5. **Have a purpose.**
For example, our climate is rapidly changing. This will bring displacement and scarcity. A new generation of consumers wants to buy into companies

---

the only person in the office responding to emails, sometimes slowly, and people can get angry. It's hard not to take it personally but we're all so used to immediate shopping, click-and-collect options and next-day delivery that the idea of a four-month delay now seems unreasonable.

Starting a business means coming up against boundaries, such as money. Stay focused, intuitive and tenacious: the rest will fall into place.

It can be hard to take time off but you need your own life and spending time away means that you come back with a clearer head. And it's easy to assume that other people are as passionate about your product as you are but it's important to understand how your customer thinks. You need to communicate. Otherwise it's a monologue, not a conversation.

I'm working on another project, Larder. It's a response to the collapse of farm jobs and aims to give a voice to producers. It's also about helping people feel confident in the kitchen using basic ingredients instead of relying on meal kits or recipe cards. What can you cook when you get home and all you have are some tomatoes, pulses or fish? What can you make that isn't expensive or time-consuming? There are simpler paths to follow but I love being an entrepreneur: following the feeling and writing the next line. — Ⓜ

About the writer: Ponnuthurai is the founder of Crane Cookware. Her new firm, Larder, will launch in October 2022. This essay is taken from an interview by MONOCLE researcher Grace Charlton that features in *The Monocle Companion*, which is out now. Buy your copy today.

with authentic goals beyond "greenwashing". Get ahead by making a difference.

6. **Don't be afraid to change course.**
I know it's counterintuitive but you will need to navigate data points that block your path. There will be many, especially in volatile times. In the long run, it will save you heartache and money to cut your losses and change tack. Doing so will also demonstrate your self-awareness to supporters and staff.

7. **Make money.**
Breaking even as quickly as possible should be a core part of your mission. If you do, you'll be in control of your destiny. If you don't, you'll always be a slave to someone else – assuming you're fortunate enough to be in the 1 per cent of start-ups that survive and scale.

8. **Entrepreneurs are made, not born.**
We are always of our time and what makes an entrepreneur in 2022 is not what made one in 2012. Focus on building your business, not your origin story, and you'll be on your way to self-made success.

About the writer: Entrepreneur and philanthropist Allesch-Taylor is professor of the practice of entrepreneurship and a fellow of King's College London. He has since invested in, co-founded or served as chair or CEO of more than 100 new companies, operating in more than 15 countries.

Working lunch
by Fiona Wilson

In Japan, taking time for a midday meal is seen as a productive part of the day. Here's what the rest of us can learn from the time-honoured 'teishoku' break.

Many things could account for the diligence of the Japanese workforce but I have a hunch that one element is the unerring commitment to a decent lunch. Not the must-impress client type, either, but instead the daily ritual of a fair feed and the fact that so many companies – big and small, lavish and humble – understand the importance of leaving your desk and eating well. While people elsewhere in the world unfurl sad sandwiches or Tupperware containers brimming with last night's leftovers, Japan lunches from a different menu.

From 11.45 on, employees pour out of workplaces and head to their preferred spot for a *teishoku* set lunch: the true cornerstone of Japanese cuisine for anyone, from entrepreneurs to employees. For about ¥900 (€6.30) – more and you might be accused of extravagance – diners can expect a tray with rice, miso soup, pickles

There's no time for languid lunches but it's still a chance to leave the office and reset for a productive afternoon

and a light main dish (think salt-grilled mackerel or braised pork).

Queues regularly swell outside the best places but tend to move quickly. That's the other business-friendly factor in *teishoku* culture: the speed. A proper meal, served with a glass of iced water and a hand towel, can – and should – be eaten in less than 30 minutes. The idea is to be in and out as quickly as possible. Everyone knows the drill. There's no time for languid lunches when there's work to be done but it's still a chance to leave the office, reset and be back at one's desk – replete but not sleepily overfed – and ready for a productive afternoon.

For some employers, the importance of lunch to morale, health and getting the most from staff might lead to the creation of a canteen. The most famous is at Tanita, a maker of electronic scales. The healthy menu at the Tanita canteen was deemed so delicious that it spawned a blockbuster cookbook and a restaurant in Marunouchi in

Tokyo called Tanita Shokudo (Tanita Canteen). So now even people who work for less enlightened employers can see what they are missing (and the business itself gets to diversify a little).

This being Japan, the roots of this healthy way of eating (replicated in families, schools and hospitals up and down the country) lie in centuries of tradition. The original concept of *ichiju issai*, one soup and one dish, dates all the way back to medieval Zen Buddhist monks and it lives on in Japanese home cooking today. It's not a fixed entity; you might also be presented with *ichiju sansai* (one soup, three dishes), when the tray will be loaded with extra sides – perhaps a little simmered tofu or sautéed lotus root. But the principle remains the same: a balanced meal served in small portions. The Japanese population's trim waistlines, longevity and dedicated work ethic suggest there's something that's well worth the rest of us chewing over.— Ⓜ

About the writer: Wilson, MONOCLE's founding Tokyo bureau chief, has covered Japan for the past 15 years and is well versed in the country's small-business scene and snagging interviews with top CEOs. She is the editor of *The Monocle Guide to Japan*, published by Thames & Hudson.

When the stakes are high
by Jens Serup

Former Danish soldier Jens Serup co-founded a firm training people for hostile environments. He shares his experience as a hostage negotiator and how honing these skills could help entrepreneurs too.

Working as a hostage negotiator has given me an insight into human psychology and I have found that some of the strategies I use in a high-stakes situation can be fruitfully deployed in the civilian world too. Together with my business partner, former special-ops soldier Norman Kristiansen, I run a travel and security advisory firm called Guardian – Security Risk Management (Guardian-SRM), which trains people in how to survive hostile situations in lawless locales and war zones. My clients are mostly journalists heading off to report on dangerous places, while some are NGO workers or contractors. Whatever their line of work, I try to provide them all with a toolkit to deal with and adapt to potentially extremely stressful situations. This may mean unpredictable encounters at a testy checkpoint, where to seek shelter in an emergency or how to behave if kidnapped by militants.

I served 20 years in the Danish army and trained units for deployments during the Iraq War before hatching the idea for Guardian-SRM. It's an unusual niche but at the time, in 2005, there were as many as 300 to 500 people a year being taken hostage in Iraq. There was a market for my services and I set

You can't have a successful negotiation if you can't put yourself in the opposition's shoes

about creating a programme for the Danish government to meet the challenges. In 2010, however, I took leave and, together with Kristiansen, started this business that adapted the training for civilians.

Cutting deals as an entrepreneur might seem benign compared with searching for an agreement when lives are in danger but I've found that above all – whatever the stakes – you can't have a successful negotiation if you can't put yourself in the opposition's shoes. A little compassion goes a long way and all negotiations are about finding a sweet spot between getting what you and the other side want. The caveat must also be that neither might

get everything they desire. The winner-takes-it-all mentality is usually a losing one.

When it comes to how to behave in these types of situations, we teach people about the need to manage their stress to assess what's happening fully and properly. When we are exposed to stress, our cognitive abilities tend to shut down and we are faced with choosing from a series of standard, and often unhelpful, responses: to fight, freeze or flee. These reactions often provoke the worst outcomes and this is when people get hurt.

So being able to cope with stress allows people to think clearly when things get tough. In our training for journalists going into combat zones, we even simulate being kidnapped (I'm not suggesting you do this to your staff). Exposing students to a highly stressful, but ultimately managed and safe, situation can prepare them.

Prior to any big pitch or stressful negotiation, for example, entrepreneurs – like hostages – must think through exactly how they might feel throughout the event and the many different ways in which the situation could unfold. Having done so, you must then try to calm yourself and carefully consider the outcomes you want. The better prepared you are, the less energy you are likely to expend on anxiety about how things could play out. Take

a deep breath. Assess your options. Consider your next move thoughtfully and with an eye on what the consequences might be.

Lastly, try to buy some time. Any negotiation is a process of building a working relationship with the opposition: whether that is a hostage-taker who holds lives in their hands or a battle-hardened CEO looking to close a complex deal while fighting on a few fronts. If you rush to find a solution, you will probably struggle to understand each other enough to find an agreement that works.

At its core, my work in hostage negotiation is about keeping lines of communication open through a crisis to allow me to seek a solution that both sides can get behind. The endgames might look different in a heated boardroom compared with a hostage situation but the basic theory remains the same. It starts with a deep breath, consideration of the other party's position and keeping a cool head when all around you are losing theirs. — Ⓜ

About the writer: Former soldier Serup is a Danish hostage negotiator and co-founder of Guardian – Security Risk Management. The risk advisory firm provides hostile-environment-awareness training to journalists, aid workers and others heading to conflict zones.

Straight from the heart
by Natalie Theodosi

Selling direct to your customers offers a level of control for small brands not found in third-party retailing. But do the risks outweigh the benefits?

Any entrepreneur making and selling something should spot the benefit of selling straight to the people who want it; the direct-to-consumer (DTC) method cuts out the wholesale middlemen. Third parties, whether shops or websites, can help you reach more people but will nibble into your margin, compromise your cash flow and exert control over the thing you've worked to create, price and sell.

So is DTC really that simple? It can be. The idea led recent start-ups to initial stratospheric success, from mattress-maker Casper to Harry's

She stopped chasing wholesale deals to focus on her own sales channel and building a dialogue with customers

razors and eyewear brand Warby Parker. All used the same formula: creating a single product at a competitive price, acquiring customers online and bringing them to the brand's own website or shops. The approach has been a success but if the novelty fades or product quality drops, then it can backfire. In February 2020, for example, Casper's shares debuted on the New York Stock Exchange below their targeted range, while beauty brand Glossier, a DTC pin-up, recently announced a round of layoffs, with founder and CEO Emily Weiss stepping down. Despite this, entrepreneurs should not write off DTC.

And there are other reasons to be hesitant about wholesale. "It opens companies to the risk of discounting at the expense of their long-term brand equity," says Luca Solca, senior analyst at research firm Bernstein. And some online multi-brand platforms are known for imposing unfavourable payment terms or asking brands to pay for exposure.

"Wholesale partners are not always the marketing channels that brands hope they will be," says Athens-based accessories designer Marina Raphael. "A small brand does not automatically get introduced to its customers, making unreasonable sales terms even harder to swallow."

Raphael's business, founded in 2019, is a good example of using the DTC model. Early on, she shifted her focus from chasing wholesale deals to her own sales channel and building a dialogue with customers. "They provide feedback, which helps me adapt," she says. Her business enjoyed 420 per cent growth in 2020 and a steady 20 to 30 per cent since.

Continuing to innovate beyond a signature product is key, as is thinking past faceless marketing with tailored experiences. Raphael regularly debuts exclusive designs, created in collaboration with people she admires, on her platform. She's also planning pop-up shops and a flagship opening. Wholesale doesn't have to be a complete write-off but a self-sufficient DTC business gives entrepreneurs leverage to negotiate better terms and be more selective with their partners.

So to DTC or not to DTC? While some may desire the validation that third-party retailers can offer, it's a risk. Going your own way shows confidence that your business can stand on its own two feet and keep its cash flowing. — Ⓜ

About the writer: Cyprus-born Theodosi is MONOCLE's fashion editor. Her beat extends from covering fashion weeks to the boardrooms of major retailers and involves seeking out honest and interesting brands from the smallest ateliers to luxury labels on the up.

Joseph Schumpeter believed that interest rates served as a "brake or governor" on economic activity and he would have been highly critical of the recent era of easy money. Born in 1883 in what is now the Czech Republic, Schumpeter rose to fame in 1919 when he served briefly as Austria's finance minister in a revolutionary socialist government, of which he quipped, "If a man wants to commit suicide it's good to have a doctor to hand." Schumpeter viewed capitalism as an evolutionary system, forever in motion and constantly changing. In his view, the entrepreneur played a pivotal role, introducing novel technologies and methods

Just as ultra-low interest rates didn't much benefit genuine entrepreneurs, so rising rates might turn out to be a boon

Appetite for destruction
by Edward Chancellor

Those concerned by rising interest rates should take heart. Here's why bold action today could create a more dynamic business landscape tomorrow.

Entrepreneurs need investment to get started and, at first glance, the historically low interest rates of recent years might seem to benefit them. And yet in 2016, business deaths in the usually dynamic US outnumbered births for the first time since the Census Bureau started keeping records. Ultra-low rates have dampened what Austrian economist Joseph Schumpeter called "creative destruction" – the decline of unsuccessful businesses and the rise of successful ones – by keeping inefficient firms in operation. Since the 2007 to 2008 crash, bankruptcies have been suppressed by the financial doping of easy money. Sectors dominated by corporate "zombies" have lower returns, which discourages innovation and new entrants.

This environment has also created a demand for investments with high prospective returns. Silicon Valley was flooded with "blind capital" and speculative bubbles proliferated – in cryptocurrencies, electric vehicles, flying taxis and space tourism. Some ventures, such as Theranos, the blood-testing company founded by Elizabeth Holmes, turned out to be outright frauds. As Karl Marx once said, "Inordinate swindling is often bound up with a low rate of interest."

of production, opening markets and finding new sources of supply. His entrepreneur is a revolutionary figure, eliminating the least-fit companies and transforming the business landscape. Schumpeter deemed this notion of creative destruction the "essential fact about capitalism".

Now inflation has returned and central banks are hiking rates. Economies on both sides of the Atlantic are contracting. Stock markets are on a wild ride. Capital is becoming more expensive. Yet it's possible that, just as ultra-low rates didn't bring much benefit to genuine entrepreneurs, so rising rates might turn out to be a boon. As Schumpeter hinted, economic downturns are the times when creative destruction is most virulent.

As the cost of capital rises, there will be fewer speculative start-ups. Entrepreneurialism will probably move away from luxury ventures, which have benefited from rising inequality, towards more dynamic endeavours such as green energy and construction. It is the entrepreneurs, not the state, whose innovations can solve the cost-of-living crisis; and entrepreneurs, not governments, who are best placed to provide alternatives to our dependence on fossil fuels. Mark my words and Schumpeter's wisdom: a golden age awaits capitalism's intrepid heroes. — Ⓜ

About the writer: Chancellor is a British financial historian, award-winning finance journalist and former investment strategist. His latest book *The Price of Time: The Real Story of Interest*, a long view of capitalism through the history of interest rates, is out now, published by Allen Lane.

CONTINENTAL DRIFT

Naveena Kottoor **REPORTING:** Leaving your homeland behind to set up a new life in Africa takes fiery determination and nerves of steel. But moving in numbers can offer a host of benefits, as Iranian, Moroccan and French émigrés have discovered. We profile three entrepreneurial diasporas in Africa.

The 21st century has been dubbed "the African century". Countries such as Kenya, Côte d'Ivoire and Ghana have been growing at faster rates than those in Europe or the Middle East – even if from a lower base. Fuelled by massive infrastructure developments and technological leapfrogging, a market of 1.4 billion people has attracted huge investment from outside the continent.

Diasporas have been in Africa for centuries – some but not all as a result of colonialism. In the late 19th and early 20th centuries, when Tunisia was colonised by France, three times more Italians lived in the capital, Tunis, than French citizens. In most cases the Italians had moved to North Africa seeking a better life. Even today the indelible mark they have left on the language, food and architecture in the country can be felt.

The Lebanese community has been in West Africa since the early 19th century. Back then, most planned to emigrate to the Americas but ran out of money and were stranded part-way. When civil war broke out in their home country in 1975, more Lebanese arrived in the region, seeking stability for themselves and their families. Many became successful entrepreneurs in the food and construction sectors.

The following three communities have decided to seek their fortunes in contemporary Africa: highly qualified Iranians who are at the centre of the Kenyan construction and retail expansion; French citizens who find that South Africa offers a more conducive environment for doing business than France; and the Moroccan business community in the Côte d'Ivoire's financial capital of Abidjan, that has become a key driver of the kingdom's soft-power strategy in the region. — Ⓜ

1.
Hamed Ehsani
(on right)
with his son,
Hooman
2.
Urban
designer
Ahmed Ayman
3.
There are
many Iranians
in Nairobi

01 EMBRACING SERENDIPITY:
Iranians in Kenya

Exports: $41.7m (€41.7m) in 2020
Main industries: Asphalt, petroleum coke
Main centres: Nairobi, Mombasa

In 1978 and 1979, Iran's revolution turned the lives of its people upside down. The international sanctions that followed increasingly hamstrung the economy, stifling opportunity for its well-educated workforce. Until early 2022, Iran was the most sanctioned country in history. This imposed isolation pushed Iran's mercantile middle class to travel – and often along roads rarely taken by their compatriots.

The Ehsanis arrived in Nairobi in January 1980. Theirs is an entrepreneurial story that almost didn't happen. For Hamed, his wife Fara and their son Hooman, Nairobi was supposed to be a stopover en route to Australia. The couple had left behind a comfortable life in Tehran. Hamed was working for his father's company, importing chemicals into Iran; back then it was the biggest business of its kind in the region.

"Settling here was the last thing on my mind," says Hamed, who speaks English with a gentle Persian accent. "But slowly we discovered that Nairobi had its own charm." So when the Australian embassy approved their visas, they decided to stay in Kenya, hoping to return to Tehran once things had calmed down. But life had other plans. Members of the religious Bahai community that the Ehsanis belong to faced discrimination in post-revolution Iran. Bahai businesspeople are often denied a licence to set up shop, for example. Hamed's parents were persecuted and the family business confiscated.

"We eventually came to the conclusion that you have to let go of the past," says Hamed. "You cannot constantly worry about what you lost; what may or may not come back. You just have to start again."

"You have to let go of the past.
You cannot constantly worry
about what you lost"

1

2

3

Hamed decided to set up a business with his brother, an architect, and today they have a veritable empire.

Now Hamed is the managing director of two hotels, Tribe and Trademark, as well as a sprawling shopping centre, Village Market, not far from the UN compound in the leafy suburbs of Nairobi. Fara has turned her passion for African art into a business, sourcing and selling artefacts from all over the continent to clients in the US, Europe and Africa. She also curates a large collection of art for Tribe, one of her husband's two hotels. Their decision to build a shopping centre and boutique hotel outside downtown Nairobi raised many eyebrows at the time, Hooman recalls. "People thought we were mad," he says. "This area was considered too far from everything."

But being outsiders made it easier for the Ehsanis to see that Kenya was changing. "Many young Kenyans were moving back from the US or UK and returning to Nairobi with a different energy and different approach to how they wanted to see Kenya," says Shamim, the second-born of the Ehsanis' sons. Consumerism was no longer driven by affluent Kenyan Asians or expats but by this younger generation with more disposable income. After finishing university in the US, the three brother, Hooman, Shamim and Soha, entered the family business, while at the same time pursuing their own commercial projects. Hooman and Soha have ventured into residential property together. Shamim manages his own marketing agency.

Over the past 10 years, as the Kenyan economy has experienced fairly steady growth, Iran's has been squeezed. Since 2010, the US and EU have imposed further sanctions as a response to the country's nuclear programme. Oil production remains one of the main sources of income for Iran but its economy is much more diversified compared to other countries in the region, such as Iraq or Saudi Arabia.

"There is a lack of opportunity in my country," says 37-year-old Mohammad Mirjafari, a trained architect from the desert city of Yazd in central Iran. Mirjafari arrived in Kenya in 2011 to oversee a building project. It was his first time outside Iran. After completion, he decided to stay. "I saw many opportunities here and very few

"If you want to live here, it's hard to find a job. The only way is to start your own business"

competitors." Eleven years later he is managing 60 employees across three businesses.

With construction booming across Kenya, Mirjafari decided to register his own company in 2014 and began importing bitumen, a viscous byproduct of crude oil used to build roads, from the UAE in Iran to Mombasa in Kenya. Mirjafari's business grew quickly: within a few years he increased his production from 200 metric tonnes of bitumen to 4,000 a year. Four years ago his company became one of the market leader in Kenya; these days he is selling to other East African countries too.

In 2016, Mirjafari launched a second business venture importing fresh dates from Iran. Today his range includes 200 different food items, such as nuts, dried fruits and spices. These are sold at 20 Carrefour branches across Kenya as part of their bulk section. "Instead of targeting the super-rich, my idea was to target Kenyan consumers who might have less money but are curious," he says. Two years ago he followed his old passion for architecture and bought land for a property project. "Iranians are used to looking to Europe, to Canada, in search of business opportunities," he says. "But slowly that mindset is changing."

This shift is probably most evident at the former site of the Iranian embassy in Nairobi's buzzing Kilimani neighbourhood. The site is still owned by the Iranian government. On the first floor of the so-called House of Innovation and Technology, "Made in Iran" is on full display: pharmaceuticals, high-end medical equipment, tiles – you name it. The products are priced mid-range, between their Chinese and Western competitors. In 2021 it was personally inaugurated by Iran's vice-president, Sorena Sattari.

Nextdoor is a massive gleaming glass cubicle, with co-working facilities. Ahmed Ayman, a 29-year-old urban designer from Tehran, has been renting and managing the co-working space for the past two years. But this is just a side hustle for him. The real business is running the subsidiary of Diba, an Iranian architecture company with a focus on office design and membrane structures. In 2020, Diba asked Ayman to come to Nairobi for several months to manage and operate their office in the city. "I had no information about Kenya,"

1.
Eric Bédier
2.
Jean-Vincent
Ridon

he says. "All I found was a picture of a baobab tree."

Ayman was thrown in at the deep end. "It was tough," he says. He didn't know anyone in Nairobi and had no experience running a business. "We entered into some risky projects – one of them was without a contract, which caused some payment issues with the client and some losses but the experience helped us to understand the market better." Two years later, with the help of mentors like Hamed Ehsani, Ahmed is a lot wiser and has managed to sign corporate clients such as Standard Chartered, a bank. "We were obsessed with importing everything from Iran but now we are focusing more on utilising our engineering knowledge and sourcing and building more locally." Nairobi has grown on him. "In Dubai, Turkey or South Africa, there are so many competitors. But in Kenya you are one step ahead."

02 EN MARCHE:
French in South Africa

Diaspora population: 10,000
Exports: $1.5bn (€1.5bn)
Main industries: Energy, nuclear power

For Eric Bédier, South Africa was love at first sight. "I was amazed by the modernity, diversity and lifestyle here," he says. The Parisian law graduate was so determined to build a life that he decided to set up a business in 2014. "If you want to live here, it's hard to find a job. The only way is to start your own business." Today his company, Yokos, produces five tonnes of dairy-free yoghurt and five tonnes of dairy-free milk a week. Bédier has fully embraced the shift from French law books to food-processing manuals. "When you love something, you can learn anything," he says. Yokos was the first domestic company of its type on the South African market and it now supplies plant-based yoghurt, milk and cheese to supermarkets across the country.

Bédier now employs 25 staff and is planning to expand Yokos' range to UHT milk for export to Namibia, Mauritius and Botswana. "The really hard work has been to scale the business and grow our production staff," he says. Friends and private investors lent the cash he needed to establish a bigger production site in Cape Town in early 2021. "It's impossible to get access to financing here as a foreigner." Nevertheless, he is adamant that being an entrepreneur is easier and comes with more respect in South Africa than in France.

"When you start a business in South Africa, there is a lot less bureaucracy than in France," says Bédier. "The cost of labour is low, and staff are more flexible. Overall, there is a strong corporate business culture."

The attitude to newcomers wasn't always thus. Jean-Vincent Ridon first came to South Africa in 1996, shortly after the end of apartheid. The floppy-haired wine broker from Sancerre fell in love with the country, but things were less straightforward then. South Africa was emerging from 30 years of isolation and sanctions, and so was the wine industry. "People looked at me like I was a strange animal," he says. "South Africans were trying to emigrate; they couldn't understand why a Frenchman wanted to move here."

But Ridon saw the opportunities in the local industry, becoming a Jacques of all wine trades, from importing Portuguese corks and French wine barrels to facilitating the flow of capital from Europe and advising on wine estate mergers and acquisitions. Almost everything wine-related became part of his business portfolio.

"In 1996 I was one of the few here who had travelled," he says. Ridon was able to bring a fresh perspective, contacts and capital to an industry that was stuck in the past. "People were wondering why they should trust a Frenchman to teach them about land that they had been farming for 300 years," he says. "I felt fairly isolated; it was not easy to enter the right circles in places like Stellenbosch or Cape Town."

Thirty years later, the wine industry has come a long way and business is booming. "South Africa now has the highest-qualified wine-makers in the world," says Ridon, who today manages a sommelier academy. In recent years, wine-makers from France have acquired vineyards here and they are not the only businesses flocking from France: about 400 French businesses, from multinationals to SMEs, now have bases in South Africa. Among them

"South Africa now has the highest-qualified wine makers in the world"

are French energy giant EDF, home-improvement chain Leroy Merlin and sports retailer Decathlon. South Africa, the most industrialised and diversified economy in Africa, is now one of France's primary trading partners on the continent.

"There has definitely been a huge investment drive from France," says Karen Longley, who sits on the executive committee of the French-South African chamber of commerce. After almost 30 years of living and running a language school in Dijon, Longley, who holds dual citizenship, moved to Johannesburg in 2012. The trained botanist set up her language-training company a year later. Its 40 staff teach English, French, German, Portuguese and Swahili mostly to businesspeople. Volkswagen, EDF and Total are among her clients.

The move from Dijon to Johannesburg has made running a business much less bureaucratic. "I only had corporate clients in France but getting paid was a lot more complicated than here," she says. "Cash-flow was a massive issue. I was busy but the money wasn't coming in. Quite often I found myself financially on the edge of my chair." In South Africa, Longley was able to draw a salary in less than three months after launching her business. Within nine months she repaid the loan she had needed to start it.

Well-versed in professional communication, Longley's advice to new French expats in South Africa is to take note of the courtesy that comes with greetings here. "The way you are polite in French is by using different grammatical forms when addressing someone. In South Africa courtesy comes with saying, 'Hello, how are you?' then taking note and responding. It's part and parcel of South Africa's business world."

03 THE POWER OF TRADE:
Moroccans in Côte d'Ivoire

Diaspora population: 7,000
Exports: $210m (€209.8m) in 2019
Main industries: Fertiliser, seafood

Entrepreneur Chahdi Ouazzani is proudly flicking through pictures of exquisitely carved wood, stained-glass ceilings and intricate plasterwork. He is one of the privileged few to have been allowed inside

Abidjan's vast new Mohammed VI Mosque to see how construction is coming along. "It's reminiscent of the mosques back home in Morocco," he says of the structure, which represents the bond between the cultures and commerce of Morocco and Côte d'Ivoire.

The Mohammed VI Mosque, funded by and named after the reigning Moroccan king, is in Treichville, in the south of Côte d'Ivoire's most populous city. It's also a symbol of the North African country's economic pivot south. The 59-year-old king is Morocco's most important politician and a prominent entrepreneur. In the past decade he has driven public and private investment in Côte d'Ivoire, and the wider region, criss-crossing the continent to shake hands and ink deals.

Côte d'Ivoire, the world's top exporter of both cocoa and cashew nuts, is the largest economy in Francophone West Africa and one of the youngest, with a median age of 18.9. From 2012 until the pandemic, the economy grew at an annual average rate of 8 per cent. "We have seen a lot of change in the business community since the king first came with investors in 2013," says Ouazzani, who himself arrived in Abidjan from Morocco almost 40 years ago, at the age of 18. "Like everyone else, I was planning to stay a few years," he says.

Back then the community was much smaller and almost exclusively from Fez, Morocco's second city. Ouazzani first ran a textile business. As the Ivorian economy grew, he expanded into selling household appliances. These days he imports Moroccan handicrafts. "It was easy to settle here – Ivorians were very welcoming and friendly," he says. His children and grandchildren were born and brought up in Abidjan.

Over the years the Moroccan community has grown to be an impressive 7,000-strong. "The Moroccan government are planning to establish a school here; I am looking for land," says Ouzzani, who also heads the association of Moroccans living in Côte d'Ivoire. "There are a lot of opportunities here," he adds. "And unlike other foreign investors, Moroccans are meeting their Ivorian counterparts eye to eye. The secret to our success here

"Life is easy in Abidjan. We speak the same language, French. It brings us together"

is that we are sincere and serious. We share fifty-fifty. It's a win-win situation." Morocco has invested heavily across all sectors of the country, in recent years overtaking the former colonial power, France. Moroccan banks, insurance brokers and property companies have all established a presence.

But the most valuable of all the goods shipped from Morocco is fertiliser. The country is the world's fourth-largest exporter of this prized commodity. In 2015 the OCP Group, Morocco's state-owned fertiliser company, opened its first African subsidiary in Abidjan. According to Mohamed Hettiti, OCP's senior vice-president West Africa, being in Côte d'Ivoire serves strategic geographic and commercial purposes, such as improved access to neighbouring countries including Mali and Burkina Faso.

But being based in Abidjan makes more than just commercial sense. "Life is easy in Abidjan," says Hettiti. "We speak the same language – French. That brings us even closer." The 50-year-old engineer has been with OCP since 1999. In the past he worked in operations and pipeline management in Morocco. Today he is the face of his country's fertiliser diplomacy in the region. As prices soared following Russia's invasion of Ukraine, OCP increased its production and launched a relief programme for farmers on the continent. This includes making 550,000 tonnes of phosphate-based fertiliser available to smallholder farmers in Africa for free or at a reduced cost. "We are all Africans," says Hettiti, insisting that OCP has a responsibility to do more than just make money from a global supply crisis. "It's in a crisis that you earn friends. Dominance is not a good position."

Encouraging entrepreneurial investment and expanding trade to Côte d'Ivoire has already more than paid off. In 2017, Morocco returned to the African Union after a 33-year absence precipitated by the bloc's recognition of the disputed territory of Western Sahara. Only nine of the bloc's 54 member states opposed its re-entry. Morocco's application to join the Economic Community of West African States is pending, but Côte d'Ivoire has already signalled its support. — Ⓜ

QUITE THE PICTURE

Whether you're aiming for dressed-down elegance, stormy weather chic or you're off for a weekend away, there's something to enjoy in our Monocle Shop round-up. And if you're stuck for where to go, consult 'The Monocle Book of Photography' – just remember to take a first-rate snapper with you.

1&2.
Doppler carbon steel umbrella
€160

Too many folks skimp on umbrellas but clutching a flimsy brolly turned inside out by a strong gust of wind is a uniquely hellish form of public humiliation. When the heavens open, you want a Doppler in hand. The firm's wares are made using production methods refined over 75 years. Our collaboration boasts a carbon-steel frame and automated open-close function.

MATERIALS: Carbon steel and polyester.
COLOURS: Olive or blue chevron.
MADE IN: Austria.

3.
Monocle 24 sweatshirt: 'The Entrepreneurs'
€95

To celebrate 10 years of Monocle 24, we've devised a line to celebrate our favourite radio programmes.

MATERIAL: Cotton.
COLOUR: Beige or grey.
MADE IN: UK.

4.
Porter × Monocle suit bag
€395

Ensure your tailored items arrive in pristine condition with Porter's suit bag. Exclusively designed for MONOCLE, it's resistant to water and scratches, and comes with a built-in hanger and interior mesh pockets.

FEATURES: Removable shoulder strap, luggage-mount sleeve.
MATERIAL: Nylon cordura.
COLOUR: Olive.
DIMENSIONS: 45cm × 57cm (17.8in × 22.5in).
MADE IN: Japan.

5.
Picea × Monocle
cashmere jumper

€570

With its ribbed neckline and classic fit, this grey cashmere crewneck will serve you well on just about any occasion. Yet its creator, Japanese knitwear brand Picea, cares about more than making beautifully soft jumpers. Picea sources all of its yarn from Inner Mongolia, the Chinese region that's responsible for producing the world's finest cashmere. But the area is currently battling extreme desertification, due to overlogging and droughts, among other things. Picea wants to be part of the solution: the brand is named after the sturdy spruces it is helping local activists to now plant across Inner Mongolia.

MATERIAL: Cashmere.
COLOUR: Grey.
MADE IN: Japan.

(+) Discover more in Monocle Shops or online at *monocle.com*

I.
The Monocle Book
of Photography

€70

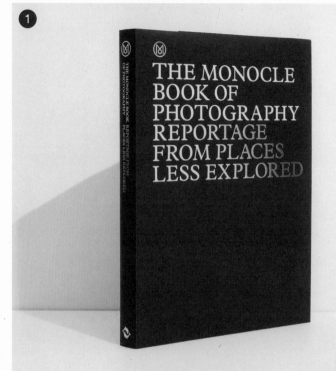

In 2007 the first issues of MONOCLE magazine hit newsstands around the globe. At its core was a pledge to commission only original photography, capturing the world on film, on the ground and in the moment. In the years since, MONOCLE has continued to document life through its unique lens, from embassies and personal residences to world leaders, cultural stars and its image-led Expo feature.

The Monocle Book of Photography draws on this archive, 15 years in the making. The book features original reporting about each of the assignments, as well as first-hand accounts from the photographers and editors involved.

PUBLISHED BY: Monocle
PRINTED IN: Italy

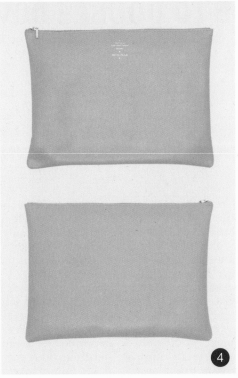

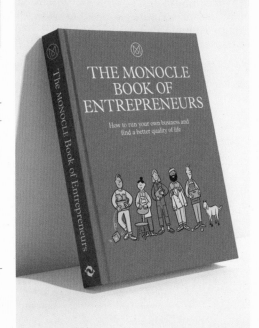

4.
Delfonics magazine pouch
€45

As part of our growing Delfonics collection, we bring you this bespoke pouch that is just the right size for all MONOCLE publications.

Made in Japan from durable PVC with a scotch grain texture and featuring branded gold embossing and YKK zip.

MATERIAL: PVC.
DIMENSIONS: 31.5cm × 24cm × 1.5cm.
MADE IN: Japan.

5.
The Monocle Book of Entrepreneurs
€40

A job for life is hard to come by but what about a vocation that helps you live well? This book is designed to encourage, inspire and even gently prod readers into taking the plunge and starting something for themselves.

PUBLISHED BY: Monocle.
PRINTED IN: Germany.

6.
Leuchtturm 1917 medium B6 hardcover linen notebook
€24

Our linen notebooks come in three sizes and all contain dot grid paper, along with ideas for living a more considered life.

FEATURES: Dot grid
COLOURS: Grey, navy or yellow.

2&3.
Leuchtturm 1917 × Monocle Drehgriffel pen
€28

An ideal companion to your notebook, this ballpoint pen, from a design dating back to the 1920s, will keep your writing crisp. It uses a spring-loaded turning mechanism and its ink is refillable. Available colours match our notebooks and it is a design object to behold, with a geometric hexagonal barrel and a pleasing heft that adds to its retro charm.

MATERIALS: Aluminium and brass.
COLOURS: Black, grey, navy or yellow.
LENGTH: 13cm.

TIME TO DOUBLE DOWN?

Running one company can be an all-consuming task but there are some who find that it just isn't enough – so they take on two. Here are the entrepreneurs achieving a perfect balance in their work lives, often in completely different fields.

Ulrika Nihlén

Photographer and co-owner of a childrenswear brand

"My camera has always been like my brush," says Stockholm-based photographer and entrepreneur Ulrika Nihlén, who has shot everything from fashion to property for a range of Swedish brands across a 15-year career. In 2018 she saw an opportunity to bring this creative eye to a new challenge and co-founded childrenswear brand Façade with her friend Petra Gardefjord, a retailer. "We wanted kids to feel free and thought that this was missing in childrenswear," says Nihlén. With its muted colours inspired by architecture, the unisex brand produces two collections a year – mostly made in Portugal from organic cotton – that are sold in Gardefjord's shop, Betón, in Stockholm.

Nihlén's visual skills have been essential to shaping and growing the brand. She shoots all the collections herself, experiments with colours and sketches designs for outfits, noting that she set out to create loose-fitting, long-lasting garments that could be passed on. "It is important that the clothes can fit more than one sibling," says Nihlén, who has three young children of her own. She splits her week between both businesses, leaving Tuesdays and Thursdays free for commercial location shoots, and then is back at the office on Fridays packing Façade orders: about 80 a week. "Some periods are hectic," she says. "We work at night a lot." Nevertheless, as Façade gained a following, with an annual revenue of €400,000, it enabled Nihlén to supplement her income while still taking pictures: "Petra and I are happy that we can make a living from it but we both need our other businesses," she says. "That said, it was important for me to still have photography. I never want to give up the camera." — ABC

Nihlén's advice:
Go for it. "In some ways it is easier to get started when you already have a business." If there are hiccups along the way, she says, "you have the other thing to lean on". *ulrikanihlen.com; façade-apt.com*

Photographer

Childrenswear-brand owner

Joey Wölffer
Owner of a fashion brand and a vineyard

The Wölffer Estate's signature rosé is synonymous with Long Island summer: every glass starts with the ripened grapes that grow in front of the tasting room in Sagaponack and more than 200,000 cases were sold in 2021. But the outlook wasn't always so sunny. When Joey Wölffer's German-born father died suddenly in 2009 while swimming, she and her brother began the process of taking over a family vineyard blighted by poor sales and in need of a

"I'm a better version of myself when I have multiple businesses on the go"

refresh. "It wasn't really making any money," says Wölffer. The siblings had to learn the ropes before taking control in 2013.

Wölffer, however, had quit a job in fashion to try selling one-off pieces by lesser-known clothing and jewellery designers she had discovered. "I'm stubborn; I want to live my own dream too, which is why I have also pursued fashion all along the way. It's in my personality: I'm a better version of myself when I have multiple businesses on the go." Wölffer began her fashion business selling out of a truck, first at society parties in the Hamptons and then up and down the East Coast. When the old truck finally packed in on a highway outside Boston, Joey says it was "the final straw". She settled into a proper boutique in Sag Harbor called Joey Wölffer, where she offers one-off finds, limited editions and collaborative pieces (she also designs and makes the Hawaiian-print uniforms that staff wear at the vineyard). A busy restaurant in Amagansett, Wölffer Kitchen, has since followed.

Managing two different ventures, she says, requires not being so hard on yourself but she adds that the businesses should bounce off each other. "I meet a lot of people who ask if I can do a fashion event and I say, 'Sure, can I bring my wine too?' Each strangely feeds the other." In August the Wölffer Estate sponsored the Hampton Classic showjumping contest, in which Wölffer competed. "Riding gives me incredible focus," she says. — CL

Wölffer's advice:
"Accept that you're going to make mistakes because you aren't as focused as you would be on one specific thing, and forgive that."
joeywolffer.com; wolffer.com

Wine-maker

Fashion-brand owner

Shin Chang and Penny Ng
Architects and restaurant owners

Shin Chang and Penny Ng met while working at a design firm in Kuala Lumpur but the couple eventually decided to go it alone and launch their own studio, Mentahmatter, in 2013. They swiftly earned a reputation for deft revitalisation projects that preserve the character of the original structure. As the design office grew, the two architects began to think about opening a restaurant where they could explore a shared passion for contemporary

"It's a place to meet clients and a prototype to show what we can do as architects"

Malaysian cuisine and good wine, opening ChoCha Foodstore in Chinatown in 2016. "It's a place to meet clients but also serves as a prototype to show what we can do as architects," says Ng. "The space and ambience speak for themselves."

They took a former 1920s-era brothel and transformed it into a social space with stripped-down interiors with iron grilles and abundant greenery, serving up seasonal, inventive takes on Malaysian

staples. In addition to housing the design firm's offices, the restaurant has expanded to include a much-loved neighbourhood bar, Botakliquor.

Juggling ventures can be a challenge but both Chang and Ng say that having a like-minded business partner has been key. Running the restaurant has also helped Chang keep "human-centric design" in mind. "People think architecture should be purely business," he says. "For us, it's about how you live your life and designing spaces for people to enjoy."

In 2018, Mentahmatter embarked on a project a few streets away, turning the remains of the Rex Cinema, an iconic cinema that burned down years ago, into a community hub for the arts. REXKL opened in 2019. The couple spied an opportunity on the vacant rooftop: they opened Shhhbuuuleee last year, an East-Asian take on their first restaurant with a speciality list of natural wine and saké. It is essential, they say, to preserve the beauty of the buildings they work on, whether for a client or one of their own restaurants. — NAH

Chang and Ng's advice:
It can't just be for the look. "We don't want to create spaces that people come to and take photographs," says Ng. "We genuinely want to bring people together." *mentahmatter.com; chochafoodstore.com*

Architects

Restaurant owners

Devon Vaillancourt and Joel Greaves

Hoteliers and concierge-service owners

When an ice storm swept into Toronto in Canada's infamously bitter winter of 2013, Devon Vaillancourt was a new employee at Zebrano, a concierge service offering round-the-clock maintenance to luxury homes in the city and Collingwood, a ski town. "Half of Toronto lost power," says Vaillancourt. "So we just dropped everything and immediately began running around like janitors with our clients' keys, fixing up issues at their homes." That

> **"If we feel the need to take a step back from one to focus on the other, we can"**

was a powerful early lesson for when she and her husband, Joel Greaves, took over the business four years later. Since then, the membership has more than doubled to 45. "We have a small team and every client has to have a one-on-one relationship with their concierge."

Zebrano wrangles plumbers, gardeners and electricians to keep members' residences on top form. "There are a lot of app-based companies out there doing this but we often know our clients' homes better than they do," says Vaillancourt. "It's a very personal business."

The same ethos led the couple to open their first hotel last year: Somewhere Inn is an 11-room former fishing lodge in the picturesque Ottawa Valley. Built in the 1970s, the building needed a bit of work and their fixer-upper background gave the couple the confidence to oversee the restoration themselves. It's important to manage each business separately as its own self-contained entity. "What's nice is that, if we feel the need to take a step back from one to focus on the other, we can," says Vaillancourt. "If we are in the process of really ramping up one of the businesses, then we can keep the other running steadily. We get to decide for ourselves how each business grows."

Whether keeping clients' houses shipshape or plumping pillows, you need to be nimble and responsive, says Vaillancourt, particularly when something goes wrong. — TLE

Vaillancourt and Greaves' advice:
"A lot of people only think of the more glamorous parts of running a business," says Vaillancourt. "But it's the details that you really have to nail down." *zebrano.com; somewhereinn.ca*

Concierge-service owners

Hoteliers

THE ART OF
TECHNOLOGY

**ART INSPIRES TECHNOLOGY.
TECHNOLOGY COMPLETES ART.**

LG SIGNATURE × MONOCLE

**ART INSPIRES TECHNOLOGY.
TECHNOLOGY COMPLETES ART.**

From initial idea to painstaking testing, our book takes you behind the scenes of the creation of some of the world's most ambitious technology products – and charts the history and successes of an industry-leading brand.

Technological advancement and product development can be approached in many ways – but the most interesting companies put some flair into proceedings, treating every design challenge like a way to express their knowledge, capabilities and degree of artistry. In South Korea, electronics trailblazer LG conceives and manufactures every item in its signature range with the utmost attention to detail. Its designers, engineers and researchers are so dedicated to obtaining perfection that the development of each product can take years. The results, including the brand's OLED TVs or its fully rollable OLED TV R, are worth the wait. In this special-edition book, we meet the visionaries behind this line, visit the company's design labs and find out why their pursuit of perfection accepts no compromise.

LG SIGNATURE × MONOCLE

THE ART OF
TECHNOLOGY

SLEEPING WITH THE ARTIST

Some hotels might show art on their walls but few have been engineered to put culture at their centre. We visit four properties that prove that adding a touch of hospitality to a gallery – or an exhibition space to lodgings – is an artful way to make culture pay.

1

2

Museum moods
Nikolaou Residence, Aegina

The Greek island of Aegina, in the Saronic Gulf just southwest of Athens, has long been a draw for creatives. Driving north along the coastal road from the port, it's easy to understand why. The pine-tree-lined road winds past stone towers, well-preserved historic buildings and a lighthouse. The now deceased artists Yannis Moralis and Nikos Nikolaou, sculptor Christos Kapralos and writer Níkos Kazantzákis all built their homes and ateliers on Aegina. "Nikolaou taught at the Athens School of Fine Arts but lived here all year, commuting to and from Piraeus every day," says Athens-based architect Theodore Zoumboulakis of his late uncle, his words accompanied by the sound of late-summer cicadas.

Theodore is showing MONOCLE around the Nikolaou Residence, the artist's former home, which has been turned into five stone-built guesthouses in a pistachio grove. The grounds' centrepiece is the airy dining room, next to Nikolaou's former atelier. Ever since inheriting the property in 2001,

> **"It was always on our minds to breathe life back into this place"**

1.
Inside Nikos Nikolaou's atelier
2.
Theodore Zoumboulakis with his sister Daphne

the family had long wanted to open the space up to visitors but running it as a private museum would have been financially challenging; turning it into a family-style guesthouse (and not a luxury hotel) allows them to keep it accessible to a wide spectrum of guests but also to make it viable as a business. "We have so many childhood memories of this place and it was always on our minds to breathe life back into it," says Theodore, who started on the first business plan in 2015 and self-funded the project (he has invested about €500,000 so far). "We were reluctant at first because it was during the [Greek government-debt] crisis. But when we saw tourism picking up and getting stronger, that all changed."

Some of the commercial expertise comes courtesy of his sister Daphne Zoumboulakis, who studied art conservation in London before returning to take over the family's eponymous art gallery in Athens. This is the first time that the siblings have joined forces for a hospitality project, a sector that they had no expertise in. "Our uncle and aunt would host friends and artists from around the island here

1

2

almost every night," she says. "We wanted to keep that openness alive."

Theodore renovated the first three guest-houses in 2019 and finished another two this summer. Three more are on the cards. "We tried to keep everything as close as possible to the buildings' original aesthetics, while adding in the comforts of a small boutique hotel," he says. The idea was also to root the residence in its artistic heritage: this year Nikolaou's former studio opened to the public by appointment. "Our aunt dreamed of this becoming a little museum," says Daphne. "We've tried to place his works in situ just as he had arranged them."

Filled with paintings, drawings and sculptures – some of which were once loaned to the Vatican – the atelier is a colourful treasure trove. "Beyond his canvas paintings, he loved experimenting with

"The idea is to help people feel inspired, to think, write and produce"

different materials," says Daphne, pointing to the artist's collection of faces painted on stones and dried pumpkins. Nikolaou's art-history books line the shelves too, ready for anyone to browse.

Theodore hopes that the emphasis on creativity will encourage guests to explore their own artistic side. "The idea is to help people feel inspired, to think, write and produce," he says. He aims to keep the guest-houses open all year; there are plans to host events, workshops and talks. "We're hoping to start a café. You'll be able to work or enjoy the sunset and eat a sweet treat prepared using ingredients from local producers."

The hotel enjoys a steady stream of foreign guests. "We love to see repeat visitors," says Theodore, who manages daily operations, having learnt his trade on the job. "At first I considered handing over management to another hotel chain or a third party but now I find it fascinating." His sister agrees. "We feel lucky to have the opportunity to revive such a beautiful part of our past," says Daphne. "And to be able to share that with the world." — DK
nikolaouresidence.gr

PHOTOGRAPHERS: MARCO AGUELLO, DAN WILTON

Seaside spectacle
Fort Road Hotel, Margate

When the opportunity arose in 2018 to renovate the run-down Fort Road Hotel in the English coastal town of Margate, Matthew Slotover, co-founder of *Frieze* magazine and its namesake art fairs, property developer Gabriel Chipperfield and artist Tom Gidley didn't hesitate. They snapped it up for a reported £360,000 (€415,000).

For Slotover, who also co-owns London restaurant Toklas, the worlds of hospitality and art are not so dissimilar. "I've noticed that many artists take food seriously as a craft," says Slotover. "You can create something fantastic from basic materials." He is not the first to have dabbled in both fields: over the past few years, Iwan and Manuela Wirth, co-founders of Hauser & Wirth, debuted their own hotel in the Scottish Highlands and are in the process of opening a revamped, art-oriented pub in Mayfair, London's commercial-gallery heartland.

Plenty of luxury hotels have made a show of expensive artworks in their lobbies but at Fort Road the relationship with art is more meaningful and discreet. A quick scan of the 13-key hotel reveals the range of talented creatives that Slotover has drawn on. The inviting sage-green restaurant is dotted with pieces by the likes of Tim Noble, Cherelle Sappleton and Mercedes Workman. A bespoke mural by Sophie von

1.
Light-filled double room
2.
Oil painting 'Hydra, Spetses, Psara' by Nikolaou
3.
Tracey Emin's 'More Love' in the hotel's basement bar
4.
Breakfast is served
5.
Restaurant manager Chantelle Kallmeier
6.
High-ceilinged top-floor suite in the Fort Road Hotel

Hellerman leads to the basement bar, where a signature neon scribble by Margate native Tracey Emin announces "More Love" over a homely alcove. The rooms feature Gidley's selection of more low-key pieces by lesser-known artists of the 20th century, while the corridors are adorned with postcards from Margate's heyday as a Georgian seaside resort.

The artworks are not explicitly for sale but enquiries aren't completely off the cards. "There are no price tags," says Slotover. "But if someone really fell in love with a piece, we could talk to the artists and arrange something – but that's not part of the business plan." One thing that the art certainly does is add to the allure of spending the night here. As Margate undergoes a creative resurgence after decades of decay – a turnaround largely spearheaded by the opening of the Turner Contemporary – this town's appeal to art enthusiasts can only be good for business. "Art is often experienced individually," says Slotover. "We need a point to come together and celebrate." — GCH
fortroadhotel.com

Change maker
Eaton DC, Washington

Born to a Taiwanese-American mother from Detroit and a Chinese father from Hong Kong, Katherine Lo's childhood straddled multiple cultures. She felt like an outsider for not being Chinese enough in Hong Kong and not American enough in the US, and often took refuge in the library. This experience led to an appreciation of culture's role in fostering a sense of belonging and later inspired her to create Eaton, a hotel and co-working company with outposts in Washington and Hong Kong. "Our mission is to transform Eaton into a community," says Lo. "It supports social and environmental causes, as well as artists."

What makes Eaton stand out is its programming. At Eaton DC, exhibitions on identity, gender and race regularly rotate within its gallery walls and its studio rooms host work by local artists. Its theatre holds concerts and provides a space for both established and emerging film-makers; in November it will host screenings as part of the Current Movements Film Festival. A radio studio at the front of the hotel makes recordings of grass-roots storytellers and broadcasts underground music.

Lo's family business is hospitality. She is the daughter of Lo Ka Shui, chairman of Great Eagle Holdings, the Hong Kong property giant behind the five-star luxury

> "Eaton supports social issues, as well as artists"

hotel The Langham. But she initially chose a different path, studying anthropology and film production. "Throughout my life it was kept pretty separate from us," she says. "I didn't grow up around that."

Lo was in her late twenties when she started to work with her father, putting her film-production skills to use by documenting the making of The Langham Chicago. But it wasn't until he asked her to help him understand the major changes in US society over the past few years – and whether she could create a hotel brand that reflected them – that she got involved. The result was Eaton, which launched in 2018.

Incorporated as a public-benefit corporation, Eaton is obliged to deliver results in its cultural mission, not just in its financial performance. Though most of its programming is free of charge, the venture has many revenue streams. "Eaton makes money from its cafés, restaurants and bars; its wellness class and guest-room bookings; its house memberships and private events," says Lo. "We take a percentage and funnel it back into supporting our programming."

The company's properties have the scale to deliver results. Its Washington outpost offers 209 guest rooms, while there are 465 in Eaton HK. Because Washington is a hub for NGOs, government workers, journalists and protesters, the hotel attracts a socially conscious clientele.

Lo hopes that Eaton will make a positive difference in the cultural life of its surroundings. "I would love to prove that you can build a socially and environmentally conscious brand," says Lo. "One that gives back to the community but is also financially viable." — AMB
eatonworkshop.com

1 2   3

4

5

6

Wild galleries
Singita, South Africa

A collection of well-appointed safari lodges, Singita recently opened two art galleries inside its properties in South Africa. Other than providing guests with exhibitions to browse while on holiday, the spaces were created to support neighbouring communities with some of the proceeds from art sales. Closing deals in these spaces might be made a little easier by the fact that the buyers are a captive audience but Jo Bailes, Singita's COO and the brains behind the project, always wants to ensure that the offer is top-notch. He has enlisted the expertise of curator Elana Brundyn, former CEO of celebrated Cape Town institution Norval Foundation, and showcased work by the likes of Athi-Patra Ruga and Lucinda Mudge. With more gallery openings planned in Tanzania and Rwanda, Bailes reveals why it makes sense to bring art on safari. — MHO

What advantages does this gallery have over a commercial gallery?
Nature has always been an inspiration for artists: the fact that our galleries are in the middle of the wilderness is an incredible integration of beauty and art. Also, having them set here, where we have some of the wealthiest clients in the world falling in love with Africa, is a unique set of variables.

1.
Where art meets comfort
2.
Eaton's radio studio
3.
Music night at Eaton's rooftop bar
4.
Gallery space at Singita Kruger National Park
5.
Jo Bailes, Singita's COO
6.
Ebony Lodge, Sabi Sands

Are some of these clients new to art buying? How does that benefit you?
It's an opportunity for us to introduce non-art buyers into the art-buying world. Being one of the most high-end safari operators in Africa, the type of audience that we attract has a huge amount of disposable income. We have a responsibility to showcase the best of art and design, and to educate guests about it. We enable them to take inspiration from the continent home. Hopefully, it will allow them to keep Africa top of mind and create conversations when people visit them.

How can you expand this model as a business venture?
Among many other forms of African creativity, art is key to our brand going forward. Elana is going to help us to create a reputation as a respected art source for collectors and for artists to stock their work. We'd like to make it sustainable and financially viable long-term, as well as helping the communities surrounding our lodges, where we can help promote and stimulate future artists.
singita.com

SIZE MATTERS

Your offices needn't be tucked away in a monolithic multi-purpose skyscraper. Whether you employ four people or 4,000, your firm's HQ can be a striking projection of your brand's values and aspirations. We visit three workspaces that get it right.

PHOTOGRAPHER: ERNEST PROTASIEWICZ

CASE STUDY 01: Big player

2

1

Light club
Fiskars Group, *Espoo*

A sign that reads "Fiskars Group, est. 1649" welcomes visitors to the Finnish company's glossy new nine-storey headquarters, designed by Helsinki-based Sarc architects. In some ways the shiny set-up feels at odds with the brand's identity. After all, this is the oldest company in Finland and among the oldest in the world, whose former home in the capital's repurposed Arabia tableware factory formed part of the nation's design heritage. Thankfully, the brand's new digs are anything but another insipid corporate office. Located in Espoo, they're filled with art, craft tools and iconic products from Fiskars' brands, such as Iittala and Arabia. "With almost 400 years of craft and design heritage to draw on, this is as

3

4   5

"It's as much a window into our brand DNA as it is a modern working space for our 400 employees"

1.
Kati Ihamäki
2.
Fiskars HQ
in Espoo
3.
Office
restaurant
4.
Floors are
connected
with a round
staircase
5.
Reception area
6.
Iittala
and Arabia
kitchenware
on display
7.
Lounge
for visitors

6

much a window into our brand DNA as it is a modern workspace for our 400 employees," says Kati Ihamäki, Fiskars Group's vice president of sustainability.

Despite its storied history as first a manufacturing hub and then a headquarters, the old head office did not accommodate modern ways of work or meet the group's sustainability goals. Not only that, it couldn't fit all of its 12 design brands under one roof. When the brief for the new building, located by the sea in Espoo's Keilaniemi neighbourhood, was written, the key was to involve the employees. "One of the priorities was to create an office that nurtures encounters but which, unlike many open-plan offices, has a sense of place and human scale," says Anni Ojanen from design studio Futudesign, the Finnish firm responsible for the site's interior design.

As an example of the firm putting its staff first, the top floor, which affords magnificent views over the Baltic, is dedicated to wellbeing, with a large terrace, yoga studio, massage room and café. This coupled with well-designed work areas, lots of natural light and a healthy-food-serving staff restaurant will help Fiskars to attract and retain talent. In the words of its creative content manager Vesa Kemppainen, "We don't need offices to feel cosy and homelike; we just sat at home for two years. Offices need to be much more. They need to feel uplifting and make you say, 'Wow.'" — PBU

7

CASE STUDY 02: Brand on the up

1

Fitted out
Pas Normal Studios, *Copenhagen*

For Peter Lange and Karl-Oskar Olsen, what started as a hobby making their own biking jerseys has grown into one of the world's sleekest cycling-apparel brands: Pas Normal Studios. After launching with a small collection in 2015, the business partners and co-founders now have a staff of more than 45, overseeing countless new items every year that are quickly snapped up by a loyal following across Asia, Europe and North America, with shops on all three continents. Its rapid growth has forced the company to move offices several times in seven years. But that's now changed with the construction of a new home in Copenhagen's harbourside Nordhavn neighbourhood.

2

1.
The ground-floor shop lets the design team connect directly with customers
2.
On the bikes in a gym flooded with natural light
3.
Co-founder and creative director Karl-Oskar Olsen
4.
Room to grow
5.
Products in development
6.
Co-founder and CEO Peter Lange

3

4

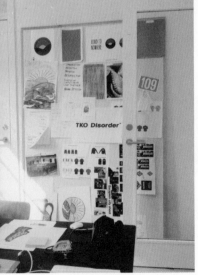

5   6

Here, a former rifle factory from the 1890s has been turned into a two-storey headquarters that combines offices, a gym and changing rooms, plus a café and community space. The firm responsible for the design, local interior-architecture practice OEO Studio, was keen to create an environment that reflected Pas Normal Studios' design ethos. "If you go through the building you'll see it's meticulously detailed," says Thomas Lykke, OEO Studio's co-founder. "It's subtle and it's all about quality – much like one of Pas Normal Studios' garments."

Those details start with custom oak furniture crafted by local carpentry workshop Raaschou, a new central staircase uniting two previously separate floors and skylights created with Danish window specialists Velux. "Before, this building was completely dark, with only small skylights," says Lykke. "This has transformed the space."

And while design inspiration might be drawn from the clothes, many of the uses incorporated into the building's programming were drawn from the brand's ethos too. Take the gym that allows the company's employees to stay fit through the long, dark Danish winter. "Our employees are very active; almost all of them cycle," says Olsen. "So the gym works for them from an efficiency point of view."

A similar outlook is taken in the canteen. "For a company with our DNA this space is important – if you listen to what people are talking about, it's only riding," says Olsen. "These conversations bring together people from different departments. It's a really good place to get to know your colleagues."

For Pas Normal Studios' founders, the building is about practising what you preach. "From a product point of view, we celebrate the hours you spend in the saddle by making the best possible clothes," says Lange. "To do that, those who are making the product should have the best possible space to do so. The more motivated, healthy and happy our people are, the healthier the company is. This office supports that." — NM

Tubular thinking
Moffitt.Moffitt, *Sydney*

"This space has won us work," says Andrew Moffitt, who co-founded Sydney-based creative agency Moffitt.Moffitt with twin brother Mark in 2010. He's talking about the firm's small office, which has been recently refurbished. The studio, which works with clients in technology, art, architecture, fashion and business, more broadly commissioned a space that reflected its polished, detail-oriented approach to design and advertising work. And it has paid off. "We now strongly make an invitation to any new client to come to our space, be with us, experience us for who we are."

The key challenge with the project was its compact footprint. "It was a slightly unusual space, being only four metres wide, with openings at both ends – like a tube," says Mark Simpson, joint creative director of Design Office, the Aussie interiors and architecture specialists behind the project. "We closed in the walls to cover their imperfections, lining them with oak shelving and rubber wall coverings, which improved the acoustics." It is topped off with Vitsoe and Eames furniture and a sophisticated lighting system. "It says, 'We are serious but we also understand design,'" adds Simpson. Mark Moffitt adds that while the clean interior architecture

1

PHOTOGRAPHER: TERENCE CHIN

CASE STUDY 03: Small-sized business

2   3

1.
Shelf-life
at Moffitt.
Moffit's office
2.
Kitchen area
3.
Furniture
comes
from Vitsœ
and Eames
4.
Breath of
fresh air
5.
Central
working
station

4

"What they did amazingly well was to capture a mode of formality in a very relaxed environment"

provides professionalism, at the end of the day the pair "are just two blokes". He says that they operate best when working in a relaxed manner alongside their in-house team of eight employees.

"What they did amazingly well was to capture a mode of formality in a very relaxed environment," says Andrew Moffitt, adding that the office's cosy size means that by necessity the team keep it clean and tidy. "We are deliberate and potent and driven in our work but the overall feeling that's created here is one in which people are very comfortable." He adds that as the day winds down, the lighting is also dimmed onto a setting that the team like to call "spa mode". "Corporate brands often talk about 'wellbeing' but we don't need to labour the point. This space defines wellbeing." — NSG

5

MAKE A MARQUE

Nolan Giles and Richard Baird REPORTING:
Designing a logo that lasts is an art in itself. So what makes branding endure? We highlight nine mid-century icons that have stood the test of time.

What makes a great company logo? If you look at two of the business world's most famous examples – the Nike "swoosh" and Apple's apple (with a bite taken out of it) – it's quickly apparent that simplicity lies at their core, ahem. There's a flexibility within these creations too – these brand marks look good when applied to all sorts of mediums and are not overly literal. Apple, after all, sells consumer goods, not apples. This brand of design came to the fore in the years following the Second World War, when modernisation, diversification and globalisation started to seriously affect the private sector. At this point companies commissioned graphic designers pioneering in a reductionist, modernist style. They formed logos that were clear in their intentions but malleable enough be used on uniforms and literature, and endure in changing times.

Interestingly, the hallmarks of these logos, whose designs could be appreciated in all corners of the world, and whose forms remained relevant even when a company changed its offering, are as pertinent today as they were back then. With modern brands understanding that their logo needs to be shrunken down to work on a smartphone and scaled up to look impressive on a billboard, simplicity is filtering back into the design process. And while a fantastic logo can't hide the woes of a failing company, what it can do, when a brilliant business is firing on all cylinders, is provide a point of recognition and a lasting positive symbol that remains stamped in its customers' minds. To show how this works we reveal the stories behind logos that have stood the test of time. — Ⓜ

About the writers: Baird is a British, London-based designer and writer with two publishing businesses: BP&O and LogoArchive. The latter is a comprehensive online catalogue of the world's most interesting logos, whose stories have been researched by Baird's team. Giles is MONOCLE's executive editor.

Motorola
1955

More than an "M", the Motorola logo is also, cleverly, inspired by the shape of a radio wave. For a company that's moved from producing TVs and radios to pioneering in phones and smartwatches, it has held up well. It's also an example of promoting diversity: it was designed by a black creative, Thomas Miller, for Chicago's Morton Goldsholl Associates, when the industry was dominated by white men.

Woolmark
1963

Designed to help the wool industry's Australia-based body shore up its relevance amid the rise of synthetic fabrics in the 1960s. Clearly a ball of wool but also appealing and distinct as a symbol in its own right, it remains a stamp of quality. Woolmark's mission now is more about emphasising wool's sustainable credentials and the logo still spins a yarn that shows the organisation's values.

Montréal Metro
1963

It's hard to imagine a simpler solution to signify an urban metro system than a logo that shows a tunnel and an arrow pointing underground. Today it's embedded in the infrastructure of Montréal so seamlessly that it can be easily taken for granted by citizens. However, the universal design language used to form this logo means that new arrivals are guided intuitively around the city.

Mitsubishi
1964

Made up of Japanese "mon" emblems, this logo is inspired by a brand of modernism established well before the mid-century. Mon designs were simple crests moulded onto banners and flags. Mitsubishi combined the three stacked rhombuses of founder Yataro Iwasaki's family crest with a three-leaf mon linked to the lineage of his first employer. The result is a refined propeller formed of three diamonds.

Tarmac
1967

Making bags of cement memorable in the UK and beyond since the 1960s, this design for Tarmac (then known as Blue Circle) is simple and scalable. It looks beautiful against a yellow backdrop on mixer trucks *and* sitting nicely on a brown paper bag. The Blue Circle Group Design Manual formed by designer FHK Henrion is a masterclass in how a company can incorporate a logo into its advertising.

Randstad
1967

This logo for British recruitment company Randstad shows how a simple, austere use of typography can generate a compelling result that leaves a lasting impression. Deploying a stripped-back version of the letter "r", it cleverly points the letterform in two directions to show the dual nature of the company's work as a brand that speaks to both potential candidates and employers in the process of recruiting.

Royal Bank of Scotland
1969

Can you spot the 6×6 grid of circles (representing coins) on which this logo is built? While this concept goes largely unrecognised by the public, the story highlights the intent of the designer to form a compelling narrative. Banks at the time relied on crests and motifs to show their gravity; instead, RBS created a marque, which is known as the "daisy wheel", that's easy to apply to uniforms and stationery.

Nike
1971

Graphic design student Carolyn Davidson was responsible for one of the world's most recognisable logos. Her reward? $35. She was later given a job within the company and stocks worth $1m for this wonderful logo, which is a simple gesture symbolising speed and grace. These are attributes the brand has applied to its range of clothing and footwear, making the logo a perfect match for the label.

Apple
1976

While Apple's second logo has morphed over time, with variations including the initially launched design with a rainbow of six colours and a later iteration using a gleaming metallic scheme, its purpose remains the same. It's a logo that is recognisable to all, with its designer Rob Janoff etching the bite mark into it to make it even easier to determine the type of fruit from which the company derives its name.

BACK TO BASICS

Ed Stocker REPORTING FROM *Milan:*
From its new base in Italy's design capital,
family-run fashion group Basicnet is
sewing together the ambition of Europe's
luxury labels with the efficiency of
American-style brand management.
PHOTOGRAPHER *Andrea Pugiotto*

1

Wander around fashion group Basicnet's new space in northern Milan and you might notice that the "village", as employees refer to it, has more than a passing resemblance to the company's headquarters in Turin. Both are former factories dating back to the early 20th century, dominated by a central brick smokestack and daubed in yellow and red paint. "We needed to find a place that felt familiar," says Lorenzo Boglione, Basicnet's 36-year-old executive vice-president and son of Marco, the group's founder and chairman. "This was a big property investment for a company that isn't in property but it makes sense strategically."

This strategy involves using the Milan site, inaugurated during the city's fashion week in September, to signal that the group is now ready to compete with the industry's big guns in one of its global capitals. The campus includes a high-roofed, industrial-looking glass-and-concrete room for runway shows and two galleries on multiple floors, which feature perfectly arranged clothes and accessories to entice buyers – another reason for investing in the new building.

Founded in 1994 with the acquisition of the historic but bankrupt manufacturer Maglificio Calzificio Torinese, Basicnet inherited Italy's best-known sportswear brand, Kappa, and its sister label Robe di Kappa. Since then it has added to its stable, bringing in French outerwear brand K-Way in 2004, Italian trainer company Superga in 2007 and storied shoe brand Sebago in 2017, among others.

Boglione has clearly inherited an entrepreneurial streak from his father, a man famed in the business for his work ethic (the story goes that he devoted so much time to his job that he built a flat in the Turin headquarters) and an ability to grow a business based on a model that remains innovative today. Basicnet bills itself as "the first marketplace in the history of the clothing industry": the company relies on a network of distributors and licensees around the world that are connected online and pay fees based on sales of its brands. This model, which harnessed the power of the internet, was revolutionary in mid-1990s Italy. Boglione calls his father's idea, which allows Basicnet to avoid cumbersome operations in difficult markets, "a perfect business model for these times". "Would you rather have a subsidiary in China or a licensee who buys your products, sells your products and pays you a percentage?" he says.

Despite this model, Basicnet retains plenty of control, with all of its brands'

1.
Basicnet's
new Milan
space with
its industrial
smokestack
2.
One of its
spacious
showrooms
3.
Selection
of Basicnet's
clothes and
footwear
4.
Executive
vice-president
Lorenzo
Boglione

2

3   4

1.
Showroom
manager
Riccardo
Miotto
2.
Display of
Sebago loafers
3.
Raffaella
Traverso,
head of global
relations
4.
K-Way
collection
5.
Pair of
Sebago shoes

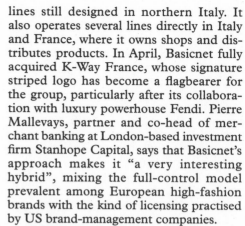

lines still designed in northern Italy. It also operates several lines directly in Italy and France, where it owns shops and distributes products. In April, Basicnet fully acquired K-Way France, whose signature striped logo has become a flagbearer for the group, particularly after its collaboration with luxury powerhouse Fendi. Pierre Mallevays, partner and co-head of merchant banking at London-based investment firm Stanhope Capital, says that Basicnet's approach makes it "a very interesting hybrid", mixing the full-control model prevalent among European high-fashion brands with the kind of licensing practised by US brand-management companies.

K-Way's buoyancy has helped Basicnet report healthy growth figures. In the first half of 2022, product and commercial licences, as well as direct sales, brought in a net profit of €10.7m. But Boglione, dressed in a white Kappa polo, is adamant that there's still some room for improvement. He joined the family firm in 2010 and has accrued several titles along the way, including vice-president of sales. He calls his work "almost a pleasure"; after all, it can involve anything from chatting with a football team about a sponsorship deal to heading to the ski slopes of the Aspen World Cup.

Boglione's father never pressured him to join the company. "There was the feeling that I had an opportunity to help him in a complex business," he says. Not that Marco Boglione is showing any sign of preparing for a succession, even if his focus these days is on strategy and vision rather than the day-to-day running of the company.

While Basicnet's background is in sportswear, many of its brands have been moving in a more fashion-oriented direction. Boglione was instrumental in the renaissance of the Kappa brand; he pushed for a collaboration with Russian designer Gosha Rubchinskiy, reviving its "banda" look from the 1980s and 1990s. "I was the right age [at the time] and had the right friends so I understood that we should let the boat go in that direction," he says. "Other people at the company might have been a bit more sceptical."

Collaborations and partnerships have become a crucial part of Basicnet's strategy, with K-Way, for instance, working

with labels from Marc Jacobs to Lacoste. While Boglione recognises that these projects have generated good publicity and have been equally good for the bottom line, he also believes that simply hooking up with other brands isn't enough. The future, for Boglione, is about moving in a "less is more" direction. "Your customers have to trust you if you want them back," he says. "You need to have the right prices, you have to put your product in the right shops and you have to do the right collaborations."

And when it comes to putting the product in the right shops, Basicnet has big plans. In particular, it sees K-Way, which is already popular in Europe, as having huge potential for growth in Asian markets, where there is an appetite for what Boglione calls "dictionary brands": heritage labels that are almost a category in their own right. The company, true to its business model, has teamed up with several licensees ("arguably the most important strategic partners you can have in Asia", says Boglione) and is in the process of opening 20 shops in South Korea and another in Japan. Despite the challenges of the pandemic, Basicnet believes that physical retail in Asia remains key; the US will be the next target.

It's time, then, to ask Boglione the question that any journalist would be remiss to omit. Given that the last acquisition was in 2017, are there any other brands that Basicnet has its eyes on? "We are very picky when it comes to buying brands," says Boglione, who must be well versed at deflecting journalistic attempts to tease out a scoop. He says that the Sebago purchase was "like a lunar and solar eclipse coming together on Christmas Day" – a perfect storm of good timing, the ideal market conditions and the right profile of a heritage brand in need of a turnaround. "It's won't be easy to find that again," he says.

It's difficult to persuade Boglione to gaze into a crystal ball and share what he sees. What's clear, however, is that Basicnet is confident about both its current position and its future. Taking back more control could be part of the game plan, according to Luca Solca, senior research analyst for luxury goods at wealth-management company Bernstein. "This model is bound to evolve into a directly controlled one," he

"Your customers have to trust you if you want them back"

says. In other words, Basicnet is on a journey and hasn't reached its destination yet.

The Milan village seems to be a signal of where it is heading. Located in the Scalo Farini neighbourhood with windows looking out onto a freight yard that will one day be a park and the skyscrapers of Porta Nuova in the distance, this is very much a vision of a new Milan, one that will change beyond all recognition in the next decade. Basicnet could be a very different entity by then too. For now it lets space to three other companies in its Milan complex. Should everything go to plan, the whole site could eventually be turned back over to Basicnet. "If one day we need that space because of the company growing that much?" says Boglione, grinning. "That would be the best news I could think of." — Ⓜ
basic.net

4

5

BALTIC REVIVAL

Petri Burtsoff REPORTING FROM *Estonia:*
For decades, Estonia's most talented chefs,
growers and hospitality folk left their
home country for greener pastures abroad.
Today a fresh crop of entrepreneurs
is putting down roots, offering new
reasons for people to sample the Baltic
nation's long-overlooked culinary scene.
PHOTOGRAPHER *Juho Kuva*

Some 30 years after emerging from the
shadow of Soviet occupation, Estonia is only
now shedding light on its stellar produce,
canny chefs and home-grown hospitality
talent. Its capital, Tallinn, on the northern
coast, blazed a trail but South Estonia, one
of the country's most fertile food-producing
regions, lagged behind – until now. Join us
on a roadtrip to take in its foodie highlights.

Day one
The drive south from Tallinn sets the tone
for what's to come. The road twists through
golden fields of corn and rapeseed, we pass
expanses of land filled with stacks of hay
and, more than once, we stop to give way to
one of the many black storks pacing lazily
across the quiet road.

Our first stop is Jaanihanso Ciderhouse,
whose scrumpy has won several industry
awards. Owners Alvar and Veronika Roosi-
maa use the *méthode champenoise*, a time-
consuming and labour-intensive way of
making cider that, as the name suggests, is
usually reserved for champagne. "Estonia
has the ideal conditions for growing apples
and we only use the ones from our own
six-hectare orchard," says Alvar, as he tells
MONOCLE about the seven varietals that the
couple grow. Many households in South
Estonia produce their own wine and cider
but when Alvar quit a job in finance in 2013
to pursue his dream of "making something
real", he aimed for the top and trained with
the celebrated cider-makers of Somerset
in the UK to perfect his craft.

With a crate of fine cider clinking in
the boot of our car, we continue south to
a small homestead just outside the town of
Otepää, where Krista Tiido is waiting for us.
She had been stoking her traditional smoke

1

2

1.
Erki Saare
harvesting
tomatoes at
Tammuri Talu
2.
On the road
3.
Krista Tiido
outside her
smoke sauna

3

Estonian chefs are staying put and starting fresh food-first businesses

4

5

4.
Restoran
Hõlm in Tartu
5.
Restoran
Kolm Sõsarat
in Lüllemäe
6.
Ravioli
with lamb,
ricotta and
chanterelles at
Kolm Sõsarat

6

Young Estonians flock to the seaside until late in the evening, filling the beach bars and restaurants

sauna with logs of aspen and spruce for our arrival and hands us a branch of fresh birch leaves soaked in the lake water. "You're supposed to whip yourselves with it but be gentle," she says with a giggle. Estonia's smoke-sauna tradition dates back to at least the 13th century and is listed by Unesco as part of the "intangible cultural heritage of humanity". For Estonians, the sauna is not merely a place of relaxation but also where meat and fish are smoked to preserve them over long winters.

Chef Koit Uustalu has invited us to join him for dinner at Pühajärve, his restaurant nearby. Spoilt for choice, Uustalu can rely not only on smoked goodies but fresh ingredients from the area, including wild venison, chanterelle mushrooms, buckwheat and plenty of seasonal vegetables. "Southern Estonia is the breadbasket of the entire country but it has developed a vibrant and ambitious restaurant culture only recently," he says. According to Uustalu, when Estonia emerged from nearly 50 years of Soviet occupation in 1991, its food culture lacked self-esteem and everything dubbed Western was deemed infinitely superior to what was grown at home. This has all changed. "It took a while before the restaurateurs rediscovered the incredibly rich food tradition and ingredients of our country," he says, plying us dishes including fried cheese with cloudberry jam, liver-and-buckwheat paté, onion soup and cold smoked salmon with kohlrabi and chive. The only mystery is why it took so long for Estonians to rediscover their culinary confidence.

Day two

Before continuing further towards the Latvian border, we meet Erki Saar at his farm-to-table restaurant Tammuri Talu. Saar's family has worked the land here for five generations and were among the first here to see the potential for food tourism. "When I opened this place 15 years ago everyone thought I was crazy," he says with

1.
Bar at Pärnu
2.
Handicrafts in Tartu
3.
Pärnu's Rannahotell building
4.
Café in Aparaaditehas
5.
Triin Vissel (on right) and sister Kerti of Restoran Kolm Sõsarat

For Estonians, the sauna is not merely a place of relaxation but also where meat and fish are smoked to preserve them over long winters

a grin. "Estonian restaurateurs lacked confidence; they thought that our dishes and ingredients weren't good enough." Saar's restaurant serves a four-course set menu that is only fixed on the day of the dinner, based on what's ripe, what fish he is able to catch and what the hunters bring him. Saar has his hands covered in dirt as he washes soil-strewn carrots, beetroot, asparagus and courgette flowers. His mother and daughter wave to us cheerily from the garden, where they are at work picking redcurrants and bilberries for dessert.

A similar philosophy underpins the work of Kerti, Triin and Kadri Vissel, the three sisters who run Restoran Kolm Sõsarat in Lüllemäe an apple's roll away from the border with Latvia. Housed in a traditional wooden villa in the middle of a (somewhat run-down) village, the restaurant serves an incredible multi-course dinner. Next to the beautifully decorated old house stands a disused former Soviet-era *kolkhoz* or collective farmhouse: an unlikely setting for such a refined experience. "We grow about 80 per cent of the food that we serve," says Triin, plating up a sturgeon with sour milk, birch juice and apple cider (much better than it sounds). The rest they get from their parents, such as foraged mushrooms, or nearby farms: the lamb, for example. "The finest restaurants in our bigger cities serve food that is grown here in southern Estonia," says Kerti. "We set up this place so that people could enjoy it here at the source."

After sampling the lamb with meadow flowers and elderflower, and chanterelles with caraway, some physical activity is in order. About an hour's drive away, the Taevaskoja hiking trail, with its freshwater rivers and sandstone cliffs, seem like a good place to take in the countryside and walk off our excesses.

We continue our journey towards the historic town of Tartu, making a stop at the Järiste winery, one of the 16 wine producers in Estonia, many of which are based

The sisters who run Restoran Kolm Sõsarat grow about 80 per cent of the food that they serve

here in the south. "A lot of people are surprised to learn that grapes can grow this far north," says owner Martin Sööt while pouring us a glass of its crisp, dry and refreshing 2021 rosé. This part of Estonia has a tradition of home wine-making and, as the region has grown into a more popular food-and-drink destination, it is only natural that some, like Sööt, have taken their hobby and turned it into a fast-growing small business.

Day three

Tartu is one of the oldest cities in Europe and the Town Hall Square, with its classical and neoclassical façades, is a good place to start exploring. The narrow, picturesque streets bustle with cafés and boutiques selling Estonian handicrafts and linen. Aparaaditehas is a former Soviet-era factory that has been turned into a hub for young creatives.

Next we're bound for the beach resort of Pärnu. On the way, we make a stop at the town of Viljandi to try duck fillet and borscht at Kohvik Fellin and to visit the Schloss Fellin, a manor turned into a 17-room hotel. Estonia boasts more than 1,000 castles and historic houses that date back as far as the 13th century, when these estates were gifted to high-born German and Russian landlords. Many were destroyed during the Second World War or fell into disarray during Soviet rule but some have since been turned into hotels and restaurants.

As we approach Pärnu, the landscape shifts. Cornfields and broadleaf forests give way to white sandy beaches. We're staying at Rannahotell, the city's functionalist-style landmark designed by Estonian architect Olev Siinmaa and opened in 1937. Founded by Estonia's first president, Konstantin Päts, the building has hosted Estonian intellectuals, artists and statesmen over the years. "It's a building that predates the Soviet occupation of Estonia and we want to respect that heritage," CEO Oliver Paasik says, as we sit

People have taken their hobby and turned it into a fast-growing small business

on the hotel's veranda overlooking Pärnu's main beach, sipping the hotel's house-made horseradish-flavoured vodka. Much of the protected building is still in its original state, restored of course. Its menu features a wiener schnitzel recipe from the 1930s.

Estonians are a spa-loving nation and a visit to Pärnu is not complete without taking part in a two-hour ritual at Hedon, the most loved of the city's dozens of historic spas. We visit five types of sauna, a salt pool and a foot bath before settling in for dinner at Hedon's beach restaurant, Raimond. Like every place we visit in South Estonia, the food is amazing – and amazingly local: moose tenderloin from nearby hunters, birch-and-cloudberry ice cream and cheese from the Kolotsi farm in Estonia's southeastern corner near the border with Russia and Latvia.

As the sun dips toward the horizon, young Estonians are still arriving at the seaside bars and restaurants, some opting for a late-night swim in the still-warm Baltic sea. What's happening here is so good that it can't be long until the rest of the world cottons on. — Ⓜ

1.
Tammuri Talu
2.
Cider at Jaanihanso
3.
Tartu's historic Werner's café
4.
Tartare at GMP Pühajärve
5.
Castle hotel near Otepää

1

Running a rural hotel

If you're ready to ditch the office job and open a small hotel out of town, Estonia offers opportunities aplenty. The countryside is verdant and full of fresh produce for your chef to rely on. The country also has many historic manors and castles in need of some care that could easily be transformed into characterful guesthouses. Labour costs are reasonable for the fit-out and staffing, and most people speak good English. Plus, setting up a business is fast: in many cases it can be done online in minutes. You won't be short of patrons either. Estonia is a popular holiday destination for the neighbouring Finns and Swedes, and among tourists from Central Europe, due to good (and improving) transport links. As the country is small, your rural idyll will be just an hour's drive away from an airport in cities such as Tallinn, Tartu or Pärnu. Rural Estonia is steeped in tradition, with people doing things by hand and growing and hunting their own food. One key will be to establish good relations with your neighbours in order to have carpenters lend you a helping hand when erecting that smoke sauna, to learn about the best spots in which to forage for mushrooms and berries or to discover the secrets of the region's homemade cider. Cheers to that.

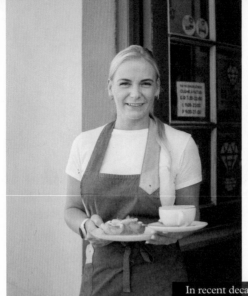

2

In recent decades, Estonia's rich culinary scene has at last regained its confidence

3

4

5

SUBSCRIBE TO MONOCLE

1 Sign up to a different global narrative

2 Support journalism that is truly independent

3 Find a wealth of opportunities

4 Become a member of a smart, international community

5 Enjoy special events and shopping benefits

JOBS WITH BENEFITS

The world of work is competitive and one way for employers to attract – and hang onto – good staff is to offer them special perks. Whether it's being able to go sailing from the office's doorstep, choosing free new footwear or taking 'paw-ternity' leave for a new puppy, businesses have learnt to be creative.

An office canteen so good it's a neighbourhood restaurant

David Chipperfield Architects
Berlin, Germany

David Chipperfield Architects has left its mark on Berlin. The practice, which also has outposts in London, Milan and Shanghai, has applied its signature minimalism to buildings all around the city, most notably in a recent touch-up of the Neue Nationalgalerie. However, architects at the studio say that Berlin cab drivers are less likely to recognise the office's name for its stellar CV than for its lunch canteen, which they regularly ferry visitors to. "If you search for us online, the first thing that pops up is Chipperfield Kantine, not the Chipperfield website," says managing partner Eva Schad.

Housed in a pale concrete building in the courtyard of DCA's campus in Mitte, Chipperfield Kantine serves a mostly vegetarian menu with a daily changing main course, salad and soup option, prepared from organic regional produce by in-house chefs. Though its primary function is to feed the studio's employees (who pay half price), anyone is welcome to stroll in for lunch or a coffee that, in the summer, is best enjoyed in the yard on tables decked out under a sycamore-tree canopy. "The idea is that it's our kitchen, living area and garden – and people are invited to join in," says Schad. "It's made for us but we're very happy to have lots of guests."

The canteen came to be fortuitously more than a decade ago, when an architect at the office proposed that a friend could set up a restaurant inside a neglected building on the studio's grounds – in exchange for cooking a midday meal for the staff. Word spread quickly about the Kantine's hearty, high-quality lunches. Today, the canteen has turned into a place where DCA's architects gather to mix with the neighbourhood's cultural crowd. According to Schad, it's now impossible to imagine the studio without the canteen at its core. "It has a catalyst function regarding new relationships, knowledge and ideas," she says. "We spend most of our daytime here in the office but if you're in the Kantine it feels like life, not work." — SRO

PHOTOGRAPHER: FELIX BRÜGGEMANN

A garden to grow team satisfaction – and practice what you preach

Tom Stuart Smith Studio
Abbots Langley, England

The green belt is a halo of untrammelled land that surrounds London, protecting the English countryside from being encroached upon by its capital. Landscape architect Tom Stuart-Smith grew up here, on the Serge Hill estate, a large house and grounds nestled in the greenery near Watford. His eponymous studio, founded in 1998, has produced gardens for public and corporate clients across the UK and Europe, and been awarded eight gold medals at the Chelsea Flower Show.

Until last November it was in an office building in the inner-city neighbourhood of London's Clerkenwell. But Stuart-Smith felt that there was a disconnect between the team's practice and their environment. So he invited them all back to his place – sort of. In 2020 he began work converting some outbuildings in Serge Hill into studios: at the same time, he broke ground on a new plant library – a garden that acts as both learning device and appealing recreational space for his recruits.

"A lot of people I employ are in their twenties and thirties," says Stuart-Smith. "Living in London, they often don't have access to a garden, so they can't learn all they can about plants." When MONOCLE visits, his staff, whose work is mostly carried out on screen, are out picking beans and herbs to supplement their lunches. Today the plant library is home to about 1,000 species, including fruit and vegetables such as aubergines, tomatoes and melons.

Eighteen people work in the studio and have access to the garden for a soothing spot of horticulture. There's a nursery being built next to the plant library, which will be run by Sunnyside Rural Trust, a charity that supports adults with learning disabilities, some of whom will be working there. "A lot of this came out of a book that my wife wrote, *The Well-Gardened Mind*, that is about the therapeutic benefits of gardening," says Stuart-Smith. His team's wide smiles attest to its theories. — ASE

PHOTOGRAPHER: DAN WILTON

An astrologer to consult on problems cosmic and quotidian

Base Agency
Mexico City, Mexico

"One day at a party, I met a tarot reader and said, 'Do you mind coming into our office and doing a team reading?'," says Adolfo López Serrano Reyes, founder of Mexico City-based PR firm Base Agency. "I thought that the company needed a bit of a boost." His idea proved providential: when the reader came to meet his staff last year, she drew cards that encouraged greater openness and better communication. Her perspective – supernatural or not – helped to dissolve tensions that had built up. The young team of twenty-somethings had grown quickly in the preceding year, expanding from seven to 22 members of staff, which had brought its own problems.

Reyes soon had two astrologists-cum-tarot readers on retainer; employees can now see them for some analysis whenever they sense a cosmic need. In part, he compares this perk to having a therapist at hand. "It really motivated our team," he says. "I understand that they have personal things that they're going through and being able to talk to someone helps."

Reyes does not wear his beliefs lightly. Even before the clairvoyant hires, Base would tailor its output to the astrological Good Timing Guide, which tells you whether it's a propitious day for tough conversations, taking action or, perhaps, doing nothing at all. "I can be spiritual but I can also be very sceptical," he says. "We started timing our work with moments that felt good and when our intentions matched what we're seeing in the calendar." Clients, he says, responded well to this quixotic yet – in its own way – structured approach.

And Reyes takes hints from the in-house astrologer no less seriously. In spring 2022, when he was advised by the stars to be more receptive to other energies and opinions, he brought on a new partner to help run the agency – and he hasn't looked back since. "The partnership? It's going great." — MCH

PHOTOGRAPHERS: JIMI CHIU, ANA HOP

A pair of trainers to kick-start a friendly relationship

Miro
Hong Kong

Some of the best company perks aren't of great monetary value but serve as a way to tease out employees' passions and personalities. Jamie Wilde and Taylor Host founded Miro in Hong Kong in 2017; their company uses software to analyse sports data for advertising and other purposes, working with clients including the NBA, the NFL and soccer teams around the world. It might be a small start-up but with employees spread across Hong Kong, the US and the Philippines, the founders need to ensure that they organise initiatives that keep staff engaged and motivated in three different time zones.

That's why they decided that all joiners should receive a pair of sport shoes. Aspiring marathon competitors can take their pick of running shoes, while Premier League fans can opt for football boots. Wilde believes that the playful perk helps Miro to stand out to anyone looking for work in Hong Kong, where corporate jobs in finance and accounting are the norm and plucky tech start-ups

are a minority. "Recruitment can be really difficult, especially in Hong Kong," he says. "What we have found is that trying to be a little bit different gets people interested." Something as simple and specific as a conversation about well-designed trainers helps break the ice with new employees, letting the rest of the team learn about their colleagues' hobbies and preferences. It's also a good way to tell whether someone will fit in at sports-focused Miro. If someone isn't fussed about which shoes they'd like, Wilde says, "They're probably not going to be as engaged with the kind of content we have."

Miro also runs team activities including company-wide tournaments for big events such as basketball championship March Madness and the Asian Games; winners can claim prizes including sports kits or vouchers. "It helps to keep everybody engaged and it's related to the work we do," says Wilde. "We have a tight-knit team – and try to have a little bit of fun." — NXE

A job for life – and a guaranteed position for your children

Trigema
Burladingen, Germany

A small town an hour's drive south of Stuttgart, Burladingen is a picture-perfect version of a rural German idyll. It is the home of Trigema, one of the last large-scale textile manufacturers in Germany. Here, about 1,200 employees – roughly one tenth of Burladingen's population – help spin and sew yarn into millions of sports and leisure garments every year. The company is the biggest in town and it's aware of its responsibility towards both its location and its residents. The century-old family business has never moved any part of production elsewhere, and in the 50 years that it has been helmed by CEO Wolfgang Grupp, there has been no downsizing. Once hired, people can count on a position forever. "Of course, if you steal or something, it's a problem," says Bonita Grupp, Wolfgang's daughter, who leads personnel and recruitment. "But if everything works the way it should, you have a job for life."

Trigema goes one step further by guaranteeing a job contract for all employees' offspring as soon as they finish school. Making this promise seems risky but Bonita explains that the policy works both to gauge worker satisfaction and as an almost foolproof way to find trustworthy new recruits. "Parents wouldn't recommend our company to their children if they weren't happy with the job themselves," she says. "And they wouldn't recommend their children to apply if it had a bad reflection on them."

Almost two-thirds of Trigema's workforce have been on the job for more than a decade and many employees' ties to the company stretch back generations. Staff loyalty has clear upsides for an employer, and Bonita believes that it is a key reason why Trigema is thriving while most of its German rivals have long since shut up shop. Having grown up in the business herself (even as a sometime model for kids' collections), she also knows the rewards such continuity can bring to the individual. "Taking one company into the future is a nice task in your life," she says. "It's a tradition you're inheriting." — SRO

A bar with fautless cocktails – on the job

Campari
Sesto San Giovanni, Italy

Nothing says that the working day is done quite like a well-stocked bar – ideally one staffed by smart bartenders trained to make classic cocktails. Campari, Italy's biggest spirits group, has grown from humble beginnings in 1860 as a company making a distinctive red herbal aperitif to now owning more than 50 brands, including Aperol, Skyy vodka and Grand Marnier. Therefore a bar – or two, as there are in the drinks firm's HQ on the outskirts of Milan – is a fundamental part of the workplace. The office was designed by architects Mario Botta and Giancarlo Marzorati, who were inspired by the advertising campaigns created by the futurist Fortunato Depero for Campari in the early 20th century.

The office bars are not just for the good times, either: they are also places of learning where the Campari Academy bar teaches the "proper" way to mix an Aperol spritz or negroni. All employees receive a special kind of bar-side onboarding – "cocktail introductions" – that the head of commercial capabilities, Patrick Piana, says are where "Camparistas start their journey." The experience of enjoying a few drinks at work – though it might make for a wobbly walk home – "means really being able to understand the celebratory spirit of the company and what it does," says Piana.

The other office bar functions as a party space, hosting birthdays and events – a sort of fully stocked meeting room with professional bartenders and unlimited booze. But only on special occasions, as Campari management is quick to point out. Technically, these are chances to "get to know the business and our brands but also strengthen a feeling of belonging and drive creativity," says Piana. Networking, then, only slightly soused. The convivial notion of workplace bars carries on in Campari's international outposts in Singapore, Munich and New York, where the office conceals a speakeasy, a getaway for employees but also for in-the-know New Yorkers. Cheers to that. — LR

A chance to set sail on the company's boats

Zurich Insurance
Zürich, Switzerland

Spending your lunch break by the lake is quite a normal occurrence in Zürich. But heading out on the water is rather more unusual. The employees of Zurich Insurance can do just that: a three-minute walk from their newly renovated office leads them to the Enge port, where three sailing boats are always ready to be taken out. The idea for this initiative was born back in 1994, when two attentive employees noticed that many of the boats at the port were never moved. They contacted the owners and offered to move and maintain the ships for free. One owner agreed – and the perk was born.

Over time, Zurich Insurance's sailing group grew so much that the company acquired its own ships. Sailors with the required licence can use the boats at their convenience, while those who require a skipper can jump on board on Wednesday afternoons, for a trip along the shores. "It has become very popular this year," says today's skipper and Zurich Insurance employee Koen van Loocke.

"I only started sailing once I began working here and had the chance to experience the joy that this activity brings." As he speaks, he skilfully instructs his colleagues to prepare for a slight turn to avoid an incoming vessel.

Employees are also allowed to bring friends along on these tours, which increases the initiative's popularity even further. Other than a great chance to feel the wind in your hair, going out on one of these boats is an opportunity to relax and hang out with colleagues away from the office (though it's always important to keep a watchful eye on swimmers bobbing along). Much as this might seem an extravagant perk, the company's idea is one of the many initiatives needed to win over new employees in a job market as competitive as Zürich's. Most of the technology, banking and sports giants in town provide excellent canteens, gyms and discount vouchers but none other can offer such offshore benefits (of the freshwater kind). — DBA

PHOTOGRAPHER: JOAN MINDER

A sauna to sweat out the pressures of work

Reaktor
Helsinki, Finland

Having a place in your office where employees can get together in the nude and hang out during working hours might sound unwise to some, but in Finland, which is a land with more saunas than cars, such spaces are a common company perk. Elsewhere, businesses may try to lure employees with offers of long holidays or discounted lunches but in Helsinki, giving your staff the chance to sweat their stress away whenever they feel the need to do so is just as important.

Companies from mobile-game developer Supercell to IT-services provider Frog all boast an in-house sauna for their staff to use. The facility is also known to have helped as a seat for negotiation in diplomatic circles (Finnish embassies from London to Washington have sought to export the perk abroad too).

Located on the top floor of the six-storey office building in the city centre, Finnish technology company Reaktor's sauna is accessible to staff members and their families. "Sauna not only relaxes you and diminishes stress but it also serves an important social purpose as a place where people gather together," says Reaktor's talent growth lead, Aini Leppäkorpi.

This particular wooden sauna is heated to 80c and the space fits between 10 to 15 people at a time. After sweating profusely in the steamy, scorching space, staff can often then be found relaxing on the expansive outdoor terrace overlooking the city or perusing the adjacent lounge's ample drinks offering to replace lost fluids.

For an international company with 650 employees from various countries around the world, experiencing the in-house sauna is somewhat of a rite of passage into Finnish culture that leaves some new starters more than a little surprised. "It takes some getting used to, seeing people walking around the office wearing nothing but towels," says Leppäkorpi, laughing. — PBU

A fortnight off when you rescue a dog

mParticle
New York City, USA

Once a stray foxhound from South Carolina, two-year old Rory now has a pampered Brooklyn life, hundreds of social media followers and a coveted TV appearance on Puppy Bowl XVII, hosted by Martha Stewart and Snoop Dogg, and broadcast to about 2.6 million viewers on Discovery+.

Rory has international marketing tech company mParticle to thank for her rags-to-riches story. "A big reason we adopted her was because of 'paw-ternity' leave," says her owner Nina Kratter Levine, mParticle's talent acquisition partner. The company offers two weeks off when employees decide to bring home a rescue pet.

The generous policy is just one among many other benefits, which also include unlimited time off. As a company that collects large amounts of data for its platform, mParticle needs to recruit highly specialised staff: developers and web engineers are so in demand that tech businesses keep upping the outrageousness of their perks to attract employees. The firm must be doing something right, as it's doubling its headcount year on year.

Chief marketing officer Jason Seeba says that they feel it's important to give employees the time to care for their new pups. "Many of the executives are involved in animal rescue and pets are a big part of their life," says Seeba. "The two weeks can be useful if you need to get adjusted to your new dog or if you have to travel to adopt. Our employee handbook makes the point though: it's specifically around rescue animals – not from a breeder."

Kratter Levine was happy to oblige. "A dog is like a child in the beginning," she says. "I appreciated that I could be there for those early crucial bonding moments." The company has always been dog-friendly: the office near Union Square has an open floorplan and there can be as many as four pets there at a time. "It's the kind of environment where you could find your dog on someone's lap on the other side of the office," says Kratter Levine. — MCH

PHOTOGRAPHER: CLARK HODGIN